CONCILIUM

Religion in the Seventies

CONCILIUM

New Series: Volume 4, Number 9: Pastoral Theology

POLITICAL COMMITMENT
AND
CHRISTIAN COMMUNITY

Edited by

Alois Muller and
Norbert Greinacher

Herder and Herder

1973
HERDER AND HERDER NEW YORK
815 Second Avenue
New York 10017

ISBN: 0–8164–2540–X

Cum approbatione Ecclesiastica

Library of Congress Catalog Card Number: 72–12422

Printed in the United States

CONTENTS

PART II
DOCUMENTATION CONCILIUM

Editorial

THE question as to whether or not the Christian community should become politically involved arises everywhere across the globe in one form or another. In the countries of Western Europe the Church is only very gradually freeing itself from the centuries-old partnership of Church and State, and this has led many Christians to warn of the danger of substituting for this old alliance a new one between "the cross and the red flag"; beware, they say, of driving out the traditional integralism of the right through an integralism of the left. In socialist countries the Christian Churches are frequently manoeuvred into the political and social torpor. In the countries of the Third World one can detect an ever stronger polarization within the churches between Christian legitimization of the *status quo* and Christian participation in the freedom movements. But in spite of all the differences, the central question remains, a question that for the immediate future of the Christian Churches, for their credibility and for their function within society, is of such great significance —do the Christian communities have such a thing as a political mandate?

In order to restrict this theme—already complex enough—within definable boundaries it was intended originally to limit the discussion in this number of *Concilium* to the problem of political commitment and the Christian community (primarily from the viewpoint of the territorial or "personal" parish), and not to advert to those aspects of the question that concern the diocesan community, or a national Church, let alone the Church

7

as a whole. That many of the contributors have overstepped these limits shows how inextricably involved with one another these problems are.

On the other hand, it was decided from the beginning that the word "political" should be understood in a very wide sense. Contrary to tendencies elsewhere, "political" is not a concept that should be limited to the State and its government but instead should apply to all phenomena of public and social significance. In this context the word must refer to all realities that have to do with the *polis* or community. Historically it cannot be denied that in this sense the Christian community has always been of political significance. Whether one takes the *tituli* in ancient Rome, the autonomous German Churches, the medieval territorial parishes, the missionary communities of Asia and Africa, the small-town parishes of the nineteenth century, the worker parishes of the Ruhr District at the beginning of this century, or military chaplaincies, one sees that the community of Christians has always had a social and therefore also a political impact. This was even the case when the community tried to dissociate itself from all political debate. (Unfortunately we have been let down by the contributor who was to have given us a few historical examples of this latter point.)

Neither can we doubt that the Christian community still retains its political significance today. It may show itself as a stabilizing influence in the community or as a source of criticism or change. On the other hand, the Christian community might play each of these roles at different times, depending upon the circumstances. It is reassuring to note that people are increasingly coming to realize that even the Christian community which is anxious for political neutrality, and which therefore adopts a position of unconcern towards political issues, attains political significance precisely through such manoeuvres. That is why it is so important to analyse the political impact of the Christian community empirically and to be fully aware of the political relevance of such communities.

But the inductive method alone is not enough. In deciding the question of political involvement in relation to the Christian community it is absolutely vital to analyse the situation and function of the community within society as a whole. This provides us with important criteria that will affect the attitude of the community. But over and above this, and precisely in the process of deciding upon these issues, the community has to reflect about its origins in Jesus and upon its own understanding of itself as a Christian community. In this respect different communities and different theologians come up with different answers, but, given the complexity of the problem, this is hardly surprising. Readers will find many signs of this in this number of *Concilium*. But in other respects it will not be possible to answer the problem of the Christian community's political involvement purely deductively. Instead, a solution will above all have to be sought on the basis of actual experience within the actual situation. *Nos autem in experimentis volvimur*, wrote St Augustine—which one might freely translate: We are driven by events to proceed from trial to trial, from one experiment to the next. Or in other words: Political involvement is something for which Christian communities must consciously prepare. It is hoped that this process of study and preparation will be advanced in some small way by the reports from Christian communities from many parts of the world which this number contains, as well as by the other articles.

NORBERT GREINACHER
ALOIS MÜLLER

PART I
ARTICLES

Yvan Daniel

An Analysis of the Political Function of a French Middle-class Christian Parish

THIS article is concerned with French Catholic parishes in the outlying and commuter-belt suburbs of major cities.

Such parishes (and by "parish" I mean all those people who go to a local church) constitute an environment which is usually made up more of pensioners, housewives, children and adolescents than of active workers; where parishioners do belong to this last category they are mainly office-workers; then come medium-grade executives, members of the liberal professions and upper-grade managerial types; and only then manual workers and skilled workers or small shopkeepers.

These parishes look back to a very rich past often redolent of strong traditions, and sometimes persisting in a network of diverse operations; for the most part, however, they tend—and this is something we must acknowledge—to be of a "middle-class" type characterized by a restricted outlook and a lack of any appetite for adventure.

Not much has changed in the operating methods and divisions of French urban parishes since World War I. Canon Fernand Boulard wrote ten years ago: "In France, thirty years of Catholic Action and of biblical, liturgical, catechetical and missionary renewal have borne their fruit: active participation in the liturgy, marriage study groups, an adult catechumenate largely dependent on lay effort, often taking place in the home, and Christian commitment ... in secular life—all bear witness to the development. Yet in spite of everything, even though Christianity is making progress in our churches and among practising Catholics, it is in retreat in social life. In other words: that vast storehouse of Christian action which represents the ordinary pastoral ministry still has no visible effect on a world which is increasingly departing from the Gospel."[1]

I. The Parishes: Forces of Preservation

I shall try to furnish an explanation. The professions represented in parishes tend eventually, if only by the very weight of their presence, to set their mark on all its institutions: associations, meetings and even the style of worship or the content of prayer.

On the other hand, the parish milieu is not representative of the overall environment in which Christians usually have to live their lives; and, most important, it does not employ the effective forces of that environment. We also find, behind or in parish institutions, a kind of "protective casing" which enfolds and threatens to stifle Christians in their parishes.

But this power of the institution, the lasting nature of its legal constitution (the "religious state" for baptisms, marriages and funerals) and the solidity of the system (a still effectively defined territory, and churches—public monuments, comprising a more or less major fixed and movable though effective heritage) continue to guarantee the parishes a definite political function.

Their own worthiness ensures that the parishes are a conservative force. All these people who define themselves as Christians, who believe they ought to have recourse to their parishes or meet under their aegis, take part in what may be called a "group life": these groups have their officials, sometimes their leaders, and a certain form of organization; on various levels of awareness and participation, they are characterized by a way of life in common: this way of life is powered by a strong preservation instinct; it is marked by a fear of change and the unknown; and it therefore resists anything new.

In addition the powers that be are happy to be able to count on anything that amounts to an assurance of their stability: for the first concern of an established power is to persist. The parishes

---

[1] F. Boulard, "Projets et réalisations de la pastorale d'ensemble", *Masses ouvrières*, No. 182 (1962), p. 27.

were, and certainly still are, a major force of social cohesion, even though today this force is relativized: for the self-image of parishes is always a reasonable, reassuring idea—you know you can rely on the stability of the institution.

Moreover, those who habitually take part in the world of the parish are generally the people who take no interest in change, other than in the sense of changes which consolidate acquired positions. Consequently they require a justification from the parishes: they often behave as if the Church ought to offer them peace of mind in exchange for their apostolic actions, or even their mere financial contributions.

Admittedly there are various movements at work in the parishes: in the new suburbs above all there is a continual coming and going. The new arrivals are often quite young, and have often been brought up differently and with different ideas. They feel less associated with local structures, and less restricted in regard to the parishes.

Hence certain tensions can exist in parishes between the forces of preservation and those of change. The institution wants to survive yet at the same time has to take heed of everything that is pushing it ahead. It is concerned to keep its members well under control at the very time when the most dynamic and active of them hardly any longer acknowledge the intrinsic rights of its structures.

II. The Parishes and the Christian Message

I shall try now to analyse the message transmitted by the parishes.

It is, of course, the Christian message: "Christ is risen! Change your lives! Tell the good news!" One might well believe that it is in these affirmations that we are to find the linchpin of catechesis and teaching, and the "guiding idea" of the apostolate. But these are combative statements: they are invitations to a permanent questioning, a change in one's life; since Christ is risen, nothing can ever be as it was before.

In fact we often find ourselves in a transition stage: we have the impression that the call to conversion, to an alteration of our lives, to a properly understood and precisely located commitment, must be rather dangerous; and so we stay at the level of asking: What are we to do? The possible disquiet is quite easily dispersed by a good conscience assumed at not too great a cost.

Here is an example from a parish news-letter (it is not a-typical): "Justice in the world. Assisting the work of justice in the world today. This kind of suggestion always leaves us feeling rather uncertain or ill-at-ease. In fact we want to answer the call addressed to us, yet feel ineffectual and indeed discouraged at the sheer immensity of the work to be done. We are soon tempted to believe that this task is reserved for broader backs than our own—for those without 'major responsibilities'—in short, for others!"

What the Lord asks of us is to be wide-awake, attentive, enterprising; not to close our eyes to the world in which we live, not to remain satisfied with appearances. It is certainly true that the distinction between the just and the unjust in so complex a world does not always stand out clearly at first sight. But that is an additional reason to get down to things and to start looking honestly and seriously. The task before us is so very important: we have a world to make more just, brotherly, human and habitable.

Looking, taking things on . . . in the company of others. Today it is no longer possible to go forward or to build on one's own. We need the support of others—sometimes their opposition, perhaps their active opposition—in order to comprehend more appropriately the size of the progress that has to be made.

But what are we to do? If our hearts are not sufficiently tender and percipient to discover unaided the just causes to which we must commit ourselves, let us remember Pope Paul VI's letter to Cardinal Roy and the concrete problem areas outlined there: urban life, dialogue between young and old, the state of women, workers, immigrants, the Third World. . . . Can we in our lives ever escape involvement with any of these major problems of our own time?

"The Master is there and calls you. Let us in the coming week spend those few minutes in thought which will enable us to understand more effectively one or other of these appeals and above all to begin to respond to them."

A text of this kind certainly does not cause a great stir. However, the document of the Bishops' Synod in Rome on "Justice in the World" (held in November 1971), the document "The Church and the Powers" issued by the French Protestant Federation (also in November 1971), and the document of the Justice and Peace Commission of the Spanish Church (23rd December 1971), have a different, untypical tone; they have not failed to surprise those who were used either to documents which were less clear and incisive, or to texts which seemed always to be intended for others, or which they generally applied to others.

As long as commentators explain the statement "The poor will always be with you" as a matter of fatality that can be seen to or compensated by means of alms, no one—much less the powers—feels directly concerned. But when Christians say with St James, "Your riches are corrupted", then things are different and it can't be tolerated.

The accusation of "meddling in politics" is soon bandied about. Regular churchgoers ask priests (whose job it is, as they say) to talk to them about God, charity, sin, heaven . . . because the rest (they say) isn't their concern in church. If their injunctions were universally acted on, these parishioners would almost justify Hughes Rebell's complaint (made some time ago) that "the praiseworthy thing about the Catholic Church is that it has sterilized Christianity".[2]

They're not heeded. But shortcomings and silences are explicable when one realizes that in many of our parishes a certain number of Catholics, most often by reason of their political choice, are not prepared to listen to the Christian message, or do not want to hear it.

They're not heeded. But their presence is taken into account—and usually more than their numbers and quality require. Yet the parishes, by virtue of what they say and do, and much more by virtue of what they do not say and do, eventually—willy-nilly—take up political positions.

III. Parishes in Regard to Contemporary Problems

Yet in general parishioners are ready to admit that forms of religious life can change, and for the most part they effectively

[2] J. Paugam, *L'âge d'or du Maurrassisme* (Paris, 1971), p. 78.

admit that they do change. They acknowledge the changes in the liturgy and even congratulate themselves on the experience. They also admit the present method of family catechesis, above all when they are interested in their children's progress; but, for the most part, too, they do not seem to want their parishes to be enlivening in the sense of providing something that will help them to live as Christians in their ordinary everyday life.

Everything would seem to show that parish people think their parish is the specialized, reserved domain of religiosity, worship, piety, charitable endeavours and, possibly, "good" papers and magazines; hence, it is as if their priests were concerned with their proper business, yet did not talk of the events of life, of work and one's job, of public affairs, of social or international problems; one might just go so far as to cite a recent encyclical (though the older ones are more suitable); but there are not many commentaries, they do not truly hit at the essence of things, and, above all, they do not instruct and involve in clearly expressed and detailed areas of concern.

The following are a few examples:

Racism

First of all we must recall the teachings of the relatively recent past. "French Catholics", wrote René Raymond, have always enjoyed a possibility of choosing between several standpoints: the 'alliance of throne and altar' accorded politically with the doctrinal agreement of traditional royalism and a theocratic ultramontanism; a generation later the papacy experienced the opposition of a liberal Catholicism of Orleanist sympathies to an ultramontane Catholicism of an authoritarian bent. Forty years later, the *Action française* put into practice the union of an exclusivist form of nationalism and a Catholicism of which it has been said that it was paradoxically the contrary of universalism. There are many affinities between integralist nationalism and Catholic integralism. Surely, though on different grounds, they wage the same good fight against modernism?"[3]

Fortunately, those days are past. But the consequences of this

[3] R. Remond, *La droite en France: de la Première Restauration à la Ve République* (Paris, 1968), vol. 1, p. 191.

accordance are still apparent in several areas, notably in religion and right up to the parish milieu.

For some decades in religious circles (and in the press as it reaches even the parishes), denunciations were common of Jews, freemasons, the influence of Protestants in the State and, later on but just as fiercely—the responsibility of democratic Christians in the national crisis. Something of all this is still operative.

Some people still manifest a racist attitude which is more or less precisely expressed according to the problem in question: the theory that the Fatherland "owns" territories, and nations, and that the Church should be their "educator"; the idea that Catholic and French supremacies are continually threatened—by, of course, "aliens": those immigrants who are now established in our country and who have been so warmly welcomed; a mistrust of the intelligent (and therefore all the more) dangerous yellow races, and of the black peoples who "belong to inferior races"; a solidarity of civilized European nations in face of the political and social movements which convulse the former colonies.

These are the difficulties which appear when it is a question of handing on the gospel message concerning the equality of men and respect for individuals, the right of nations to control their own affairs and develop normally, the morality of colonial wars which just go on and engulf entire countries, the way to treat displaced persons, migrants and foreign workers with special work legislation, with specially adapted labour laws.

In France there was clear evidence in the case of Indo-China (and then of Algeria) of torture, and then there are the circumstances of foreigners in some areas of our big cities: many people in our parishes were ready to help in providing education, social or charitable assistance; but very few of them were prepared to go back to the causes, since they would then be led to make a political judgment—which is something they undoubtedly do not want.

Justice and Peace in the World

There is a certain reassuring way of treating a subject which seems easily to get rid of the difficulties. However, for some years all those events which grip the developing countries and set problems for them have made Christians show their new awareness. In regard to nations this is a matter of a liberating demand for justice; political regimes are spoken of as being in a "state of mortal sin"; one hears talk of the rights of their peoples against oppressions and against economic enslavement, whether emanating from the governments in question themselves, or from outside. Peace in the world is to be had at the price of the beginning of justice.

It is necessary to return to certain statements made by the episcopal conference of Peru, issued on 3rd September 1971 and published at the time in the press: "The Gospel announced so authentically to the oppressed necessarily has a function as what might be called 'conscientization'. It helps them to see their quality as individuals, their situation as the dispossessed, and the injustice in which they are placed. It commits them to fight against that situation and that injustice.

"Work legitimately and primarily entitles men to property. It is therefore necessary to go beyond approval of the means of production, and to promote a form of social property.

"We wish the Synod to denounce the pseudo-neutrality of those countries which, by means of their banking systems, favour the flight, accumulation and protection of capital while putting into practice a course of political action which impoverishes countries like ours.

"We propose that the national Churches of powerful countries censure the sale of arms to countries of the Third World and denounce nuclear armaments."

It is difficult to speak of peace and justice since one has then to deal with Church-State relations, and concordats, whether official or unofficial; one also touches on problematic subjects: opposition to military budgets and the armaments race; traffic in arms from machine-guns to aeroplanes and missiles; legislation permitting conscientious objection; really effective aid for impoverished countries, the control of grants, the exploitation of local resources by the producer countries themselves; co-operative efforts.

In this way it is possible to get at the nerve centres of power. As for those parishioners who read this or that paper, listen to the radio, regularly watch television and above all have been brought up in a state of unconditional respect for the established order (looked on as a virtue), they do not understand that such problems are being broached; they do not accept any necessary indication of these viewpoints. For them that is all "politics"; they forget that when they speak in this way they are already practising politics. They forget their Christian duty, which is to examine their political options in the light of the Gospel and of their faith; in this way they mortgage the witness due from their parishes.

Socialist Options

On 1st May 1972 the French bishops of the "Episcopal Commission on the Working World" published a document entitled "The first stage in an analysis by the Bishops' Commission on the working world in dialogue with Christian militants who have made the choice of Socialism".[4] There has been much subsequent comment on this document. All such reactions reveal a latent state of mind which ultimately finds expression in behaviour.

For unsubtle traditionalists, it is a matter for regret that such a document should ever have been published: its intention may be to indicate the relations that Christians may have with Socialism, but it contains naïvetés, illusions and errors. Before anything else, one has to "think as a Christian", and militant Christian workers ought to be better informed about Socialism—both lucidity and competence are attacked in order to diminish credibility.

Other commentators underline the fact that the document worries a considerable number of Christians. They are distressed at what they see as an amalgamation of the promotion of social justice with (what they believe to be) an explicit appeal to Socialist ideology. They remind us that the popes condemned all forms of Socialism because Socialisms are said to claim that human imperfections derive from society, and that it is therefore possible to found a perfect society—one in which men would be perfect. They add the judgment that the condemnation of Marxism was particularly clear in view of the importance of this doctrine everywhere today, but that the condemnation of Social-

[4] Text published in *Documentation catholique*, No. 1609 (21st May 1972), p. 471.

ism as contrary to human nature—to man as a person—has never varied from the middle of the nineteenth century to the present.

For more categorical individuals, Socialism is the "devil", whereas capitalism represents order, success through work, which is said to be compatible with religion. Socialist politics, the politics of the left, apparently, is "diabolic" too, because the politics of the right, or the politics of the centre, are tendencies admissible in the Church.

For the more diplomatic, Socialism with a happy face is a hypothesis which always requires a form of verification that the facts make increasingly dubious. They state this as if a favourable verification of capitalism had already for the most part satisfied their Christian conscience.

In fact, the document marks the questioning of that actual alliance which has existed for more than a century between capitalism and the Christian world. This alliance is now rejected by an increasing number of Christians who express ever more emphatically their dissatisfaction with the inadequate recognition accorded to human rights in the system we know and in the face of the lasting nature of increasingly large economic and social inequalities.

Now, however, the bishops recognize that Christians are committed—and not ideologically—to Socialist options, and enter into dialogue with them. This is important, since up to now it was the so-called "managerial" circles (in France, not Socialist) that usually came into contact with the bishops. It would seem that this monopoly has ceased to exist. Perhaps the change has been noticed.

In addition, it is necessary to reveal the history of relations between the Church and the working-classes. At the time of Popes Leo XIII and Pius XI an interest was taken in the working-class world and descriptions offered of its disadvantaged situation, the problems it raised, and how these questions ought to be answered. Since then, with Popes John XXIII and Paul VI, with the Second Vatican Council, people have been looking for the cause of working-class tragedies, and there has been a realization that the working-class is the first victim of an economic system based on money and profit; a beginning has been made in criticizing and thus opposing the abuses of capitalism.

This analysis is not obvious for many people in the parishes, nor is the diagnosis made of the economic system which controls us: this is clear from the correspondence columns of Catholic newspapers—for example, *La Croix*, which has also published recently some very interesting accounts of the subject.

But this negative behaviour partly impedes pastoral work; it is understandable that, faced with largely unimaginative criticisms, the bishops have had to offer some kind of response.[5] Certain French Catholic circles consider it sufficient that the social teaching of the Church should have been enunciated in an unchangeable form, even if in the last century and in different circumstances.

Increasingly, however, there is evidence of a pastoral policy oriented towards Christians' actual lives—one that explains commitment—even political commitment—as having something to do with their faith.

This does make some people change churches, but a movement in the opposite direction is noticeable too: there are Christians who separate from parishes where nothing is said, nothing is done, and no position is taken up in regard to anything. This is very much one of the reasons for the present disaffection of Christians to their parishes: they do not experience them as communities where their faith can breathe freely or their active efforts could be usefully applied in common.

In conclusion, we must hope that parishes will recognize as legitimate and even as useful the diversity of Christian political and social commitments; that they will help and support those who take responsibility for such commitments. It is not merely a question of solidarity between Christians, but of the collective witness of Christians; so that they keep their feet on the ground and recognize that political and social struggle is necessary if we are to make sure of a more just form of organization—even though the ultimate and essential aim is the charity of the Gospel.

Translated by John Griffiths

---

[5] See "Réflexions sur un dossier", by Mgr Maziers, Archbishop of Bordeaux, *Documentation catholique*, No. 1612 (7th July 1972), p. 623.

Robert Delaney

Analysis of the Political Function of a Christian Community in Panama

ON 11 October 1968 a military coup abruptly overthrew Panama's president, and some two weeks later a march protesting the new dictatorship radically altered the historical role of an ecclesial community there, making it a symbol of courage and civic responsibility for the entire country. After demonstrations had been suppressed at the National University no other organized challenge materialized. Nevertheless, the parishioners of San Miguelito, a poor suburb outside of Panama City, defying the prohibition of assembly, met secretly in their homes and in the parish centre to formulate a programme of confrontation. The lay leaders of the parish had long been accustomed to organizing "neighbourhood programmes" of evangelization in the homes, since the guiding principles in founding the San Miguelito pastoral experiment by three diocesan priests from Chicago in 1963 were that Church exists only where a true community inspired by a common faith exists, and that this church community comes into being at the same time as the emergence of local leadership.

I. FORMATION

As a consequence of this people-centred policy the mission was subdivided as new communities were created, resulting in six parishes, each composed of many "neighbourhood mini-churches" or basic communities with their own non-ordained charismatic co-ordinators. These lay ministers, called *Hermanos* (Brothers), were the single most important factor in the evangelization of over 8,000 adults on a small group dialogue basis. Before long the *Hermanos* assumed many roles usually reserved to priests: preaching, distribution of Communion, administration of the parishes as well as missionizing outside districts. Some of these men were incorporated into the pastoral team as full-time, paid missionaries. Gradually, through a system of parish councils, women too began to participate in pastoral planning and evangelization.

In 1967 a secular organization, *MUNDO* (Movement for National Unification, Development and Orientation), was created to promote such socio-economic works as co-operatives, credit unions, trade schools and adult education. Although secular, *MUNDO* was run by men formed as *Hermanos*, and it reflected the general mentality of the priests of change through development, a position which promoters of the theology of liberation now judge as insufficient because it does not promote radical structural change.

II. Confrontation

With this background the men and women of San Miguelito met secretly with the priests in their homes in the days following the 1968 revolution. Fr Leo Mahon, the leader of the priest team, was a guiding influence, but it was the laymen themselves who made the final decision to confront the new head of government, General Omar Torrijos. In a letter they demanded a restoration of democratic procedures, threatening otherwise to stage a protest march. No response was given, and more than 1,000 persons gathered in the parish centre on the evening of 18 October, committing themselves to make a public act of solidarity with all Panamanians desiring a free country. A biblical passage describing the Israelites standing before the Red Sea was read: "Moses answered the people, 'Have no fear! Stand firm and you will see what Yahweh will do to save you today: the Egyptians you see today, you will never see again. Yahweh will do the fighting for you: you have only to keep still.' Yahweh said to Moses, 'Why do you cry to me so? Tell the sons of Israel to march on'" (Exodus 14. 13 ff.). The Bible was closed and the people marched arm in arm in a silent candlelight procession with the *Hermanos* in the lead, accompanied by Fr Mahon carrying a cross. On the outskirts of the capital 200 armed soldiers confronted them, ordering them to disperse. One of the leading *Hermanos* spoke up immediately: "You can't speak to us like that; we are a formed people!" Then a demand for the restoration of democracy was presented and the procession was allowed to continue.

In the next few days leading government officials came to the parish centre seeking to intimidate the leaders and threatening reprisals. Finally, a compromise was reached. Many delays followed so that the people again took the initiative gradually formulating the "Pilot Plan of San Miguelito", a formula for the self-determination of their region. This was to be accomplished in four steps: (1) The more than a hundred different sociopolitical societies of the San Miguelito area would be organized into a single representative body to inspire discipline and identity as a community. (2) A technical analysis of the problems of the region would be made and a programme of development drawn up. (3) A "dialogue course" would then be offered to the entire adult population to form and orientate them towards self-government. (4) Finally, a massive plan to educate the adults would be undertaken to ensure maximum understanding and participation by the people.

General Torrijos, impressed both by the maturity of the people and the organizing ability of Fr Mahon, approved the Plan. To ensure experienced leadership most of the responsible men were chosen from among the *Hermanos* and organizers of *MUNDO*. "Thus", said Eric de Leon, one of the chief architects of the Plan, "in its very beginnings the Plan was a rare example of combining the efforts of the three elements of our society: Government, Church and Community. We are convinced that the initial great success of the Plan was due precisely to this combination of efforts."[1]

For more than a year the General actively supported the programme even though factions within the government systematically opposed it. Provisional leaders were elected and a massive programme entitled "Dialogues for Freedom" was conducted in every district. The parish leaders became so deeply involved that

[1] "San Miguelito, Fracaso o Reto?", *Diálogo Social*, 28 (1971), p. 12.

all normal evangelization programmes were suspended, occasioning a serious crisis within the community. Many claimed the Church had abandoned evangelization in favour of politics. Up to one-third of the *Hermanos* withdrew, and a year later further policy differences prompted the four Maryknoll nuns working on the team to leave. All this seems to indicate that the planning and decisions were being made more by an élite at the top than by a broad consensus at the bottom. Nevertheless, two factors must be considered: first, the revolution caught everyone unprepared and this single opportunity to transform it into something positive demanded a total commitment; second, the majority of the people were not prepared for the abrupt policy change on the part of the priests who had formerly taught that there was a definite separation between evangelization and humanization.

III. Popular Elections

On 16 August 1970 popular elections, which were forbidden elsewhere in the nation, were held in San Miguelito. Sixty-five per cent of those registered voted, and on 1 September the first mayor was installed. For people accustomed to violence and fraud in politics, this peaceful election was an accomplishment. The entire region with a population of 75,000 was divided into 15 areas with elected representatives for each, and these in turn were subdivided into 68 sectors also with representatives. It was insisted that the elected officials attend dialogue courses stressing the ideals of service and honesty for those in authority. The competence of the parishioners conducting the dialogues for freedom was so recognized by the voters that 60% of the officials elected were from among these men, although the parish makes up only 10% of the general population.

Many needed public works were initiated and a unique system of local courts began functioning. Arbitrators were elected in each sector to function without pay as judges at a weekly court where local disputes could be resolved on a voluntary basis in a spirit of reconciliation and compromise. This effective instrument in educating the people to resolve their problems amicably is an outstanding realization of Fr Mahon's fundamental principle that people become free by accepting responsibility. When this occurs at the very base of society, new structures are created by which the people can consciously participate in determining their own destiny.

IV. Expansion

Because of the responsible self-determination manifested by the community, the mayor was able to negotiate special low interest loans for development: $4,700,000 from the U.S.A. and $3,000,000 from West Germany. These funds were destined for a widespread housing project and for a unique public development organization to promote and regulate commercial, industrial and other services which were to be owned in part by the municipality, by the residents and by the workers. The committee representing these three groups was to ensure that all function for the common good of the whole society. Fr Mahon described the experiment in these terms: "In San Miguelito there appears to be emerging a new vision of man and of his society which rejects both capitalism and Marxism, and is a great thrust forward towards what we could call 'communitarianism'. It appears as a movement of profound changes based on faith in men committed to a free process of creation, a movement which will have a radical effect on the structures of the Church, of the government and of the economic system."[2]

On several occasions General Torrijos was equally praising in his comments: "San Miguelito is an experiment and a laboratory. I believe that we are doing it well and I have faith in the success of this experiment. Its favourable results will be applied to the rest of the Republic."[3]

V. Betrayal

These promises were never realized. In January 1971 a major government agency refused further co-operation with the Plan. In June a priest working in another part of Panama was abducted and presumably murdered. Vigorous protests by Church authorities resulted in a crisis of national proportions during which the government resorted to suppression, intimidation and threats of

[2] *Op. cit.*, p. 5.   [3] *Op. cit.*, p. 20.

expulsion against six priests of whom the prime target was Fr Mahon. The parish was referred to as a centre of subversion and counter-revolution. In August two foreign community developers were expelled. In September the mayor of San Miguelito was deposed and all efforts to restore a representative local government have failed.

The church community, hindered from external expression, concentrated its attention on its own internal recovery, plus new programmes of humanization with a much broader scope than ever before. As of January 1972 an extensive plan of adult education was begun directed at the six great problem areas most often impeding individuals from achieving their full human destiny: religion, the family, sex, education, politics and economy. Each ten-week series of dialogues concentrates on one of these themes, challenging the participants to commit themselves to humanize their society. Unique to these dialogues is that conversion to the church community is no longer the primary goal, and therefore the humanization process is not made a condition of religious affiliation, although it is the conviction of the pastoral team that to become a Christian is to become a man in the fullest sense.

This marks another in a long series of developments in the self-understanding of the Church in San Miguelito and of its mission. In ten years it has evolved from a priest-directed experimental parish to a communally directed, mission oriented local Church, and then, especially after the revolution, it understands itself no longer as "the community", but rather as "the movement", the humanizing leaven, within the whole social-civic complex of San Miguelito which is "the community". The objective is to create an authentically human society, one serving as a model, "the seed of a new culture" for the rest of Panama.

Critics believe that this movement is still far from its goal, too reformist in confronting the military-capitalistic power structure oppressing the masses, and still not "Panamanian" because of its continued dependence on the Church in the United States in its economy and its personnel. Others consider it to be an ideological island developed in isolation from the Panamanian and Latin American reality.

There is some truth in each of these charges and there are still other ambiguities within the movement itself. However, Latin

American society and the Church at large are also full of ambiguities. This local Church is certainly not the last word in post-conciliar development nor is it as radical as the theologians of liberation insist is necessary to effect the structural changes needed.

However, San Miguelito is in process, and it represents a stage of maturity, conscientization and politization rarely achieved in such a cross-section of society. There is every indication that its history has not reached its final stage. On the contrary, the crushing intervention of the military has brought new, more critical programmes into being in a situation where direct revolution would be fruitless and where no just reforms can be expected from the ruling powers.

There are many roads to liberation but none that does not involve a multi-staged process of growth and conscientization. Precisely in this respect have the People of God in San Miguelito made an important contribution. The growth in their own self-understanding through a long series of crises and successes is in itself a visible sign that the Church, like society in general, or more fundamentally like man himself, is in the process of becoming. That discovery is critical for the Church in order to comprehend its relationship to the rest of society, to see itself as a movement for the humanization of the social community.

San Miguelito provides one such concrete example to serve as a model for reflection, a point of departure or a sign of contradiction, depending upon how it is interpreted. Be that as it may, it does provide an on-going testimony seldom achieved by an ecclesial community. Before the end of the decade its population will have expanded from 75,000 to 200,000, making San Miguelito the second largest city of Panama. Even under the present repressive circumstances the local Church continues to inspire a hope and a means for a better life which is good news to the oppressed, and it may yet designate a turning-point in Panama's history, becoming in fact the seed of a new culture.

José-Maria González-Ruiz

The Political Meaning of Jesus in the Christian Community's Political Commitment

IN THE gospels, Jesus does not appear as a truly national public figure in the Palestine of his time. He appears as a provincial prophet who did not have a great influence on the majority of his fellow countrymen. In that case, E. Trocmé asks,[1] how can we explain his condemnation by the highest court in the land and his execution by the Romans in Jerusalem? One thing only is certain, that the Roman power in Palestine condemned Jesus to crucifixion under strong pressure from the nationalist authorities. This must be our starting-point for an outline of the political meaning of Jesus.

I. The Christology of the "Son of Man": its Political Meaning

Firstly, we should not forget that, in Jesus' historical context, the religious aspect and even more the aspect of the Church was closely bound up with the political aspect. From the synoptic gospels we see clearly Jesus' deliberate intentions for his chosen group of disciples and the work he meant them to do both in Israel and abroad. These intentions form the basis of a political profile of Jesus, for both his own inner intentions and the interpretation given to them by the people and the Jewish and Roman authorities.

The first written gospel, Mark, gives us valuable insight into

[1] *Jésus de Nazareth vu par les témoins de sa vie* (Neuchâtel, 1971), p. 125.

31

the position taken by Jesus with regard to politics. In particular, the use of the term "Son of Man". Today there is general agreement that Jesus' use of this expression is related to its usage in late Judaism to mean some sort of eschatological saviour.

Our first text is Daniel 7. 13–14. The figure of "the Son of Man" recurs in other texts of late Judaism. In the apocalyptic work known as the "Fourth Book of Esdras" the Son of Man rises from the waves of the sea and walks on the clouds like a saviour (Chapter 13). It is said of him that the Most High has been keeping him in readiness for a great time, to save creation through him. He is also expressly called the "Messiah".

But the figure of the Son of Man appears most clearly in Chapters 37–41 of the Ethiopian Book of Enoch. This late Jewish work is very important for the understanding of the beginnings of Christianity. The most important chapters on the "Son of Man" are 46, 48 f., 52, 62, 69, 71. Here the Son of Man appears as one whose name was spoken by the "Ancient of Days" at the beginning of creation. In this book, too, the "Son of Man" is expressly called the "Messiah".

In short, in the time of Jesus, the figure of the Son of Man was current among the Jews as an important person in the history of Israel, bearing a special relationship to God, whose prophet and even "Messiah" he is. We restrict ourselves here to the gospel of Mark, in which the expression "Son of Man" recalls the classic figure of apocalyptic literature, particularly Daniel, Esdras and Enoch.)

In Daniel 7 the "Son of Man" is set against "four beasts" expressly stated to be four mighty empires. He who has been sent by God, who will obtain the final victory over these powers, is described, on the contrary, as having a "human face"—he is the "Son of Man", man, a human being. The opposition is plain. Throughout the Bible, "power" is regarded as a sort of "demoniac space". This is why the great empires, the great powers of the world are represented as wild beasts. Those who represent God, on the other hand, have a human face. The prophet, the "Messiah", the Lord's anointed, although sent by God, is always a man, within reach of all men. He is also a suffering man; the "suffering servant of God" of Trito-Isaiah combines easily with the "Son of Man".

In Mark, when Jesus calls himself the "Son of Man" he is nearly always referring to the suffering and contempt that men, particularly the powerful, will inflict on him and which he will bear in a spirit of service to mankind (Mk. 9. 9, 12; 10. 35; 13. 26; 14. 21, 62). The "Son of Man" is always presented as sent by God who will do his mighty work in his name and overthrow all the "beasts". But this victory will be "eschatological". The "Son of Man", although he comes on earth and shares the life of men, does not have as his mission to offer an alternative to the "powers" *here*, on earth, within history. However, he is already fighting the beasts. But in God's plan the "beasts" will continue in power, and often against the "Son of Man" and his people, and only at the end of human history, when God interrupts, will the "Son of Man" take possession of the kingdom of God. Then all the "beasts" will be put down for ever.

We can see that the expression "Son of Man" stresses the renunciation of all historical power by him whom God has sent. This "power" has been given by God to the beasts to satisfy their hungry arrogance and pride. The "Son of Man" and his people, his "community", must always keep their distance from the demoniac space of this "power".

We should not forget that the apocalyptic books in which this figure of the Son of Man appears against the beasts were written in times of persecution, and so use symbolic language to protect themselves. The "people of God" persecuted by the "beasts" did not try to overthrow them immediately and replace them by a more "human" power. They used the situation to make clearer the "eschatological" nature of God's victory. This apocalyptic tradition was in full force in the time of Jesus and continued into primitive Christianity. Thus the New Testament also has its "apocalypse". In the Apocalypse of John, for example, Jesus reappears as the "Son of Man" in *eschatological* power (Apoc. 1. 12–13, 17–18; 14. 14).

Jesus' use of the term "Son of Man" is intended as an authentic and exclusive interpretation of his messianic function. Among the Jews of his day the "Messiah" was expected to be a political saviour. He would be a leader of Israel, to free them from the powers occupying Solomon's ancient kingdom. On the other hand the "Son of Man" will only come into his power beyond human history. However, the "Son of Man" and his people do not withdraw from human history, they take an active part in its development in their unceasing struggle to keep and develop a *human face* in a world ruled by successive "beasts". But, we must repeat, the Son of Man and his people must renounce for ever the greatest of all temptations, that of offering a concrete alternative to the power of the beasts, a Christian Kingdom of this world.

II. Ecclesiology of the "Son of Man"

The evangelists give us a certain christology with its parallel ecclesiology. Thus the concept "Son of Man" which was clearly at the centre of Jesus' historical consciousness, is logically reflected in the type of "community", which Jesus himself founded, and the commands which he gave it. Jesus founded a unique community, which did not reproduce its Jewish models. To begin with, we may say that Jesus founded a community that could not even be called a democracy.

Democracy is a political system, in which all social power comes solely from the "people". In the Athenian democracy the "people" were only the free men, although slaves were of course the majority of the population. In modern terms, "formal democracy" gets its real power from the forces of capital, which is able to mount an effective electoral campaign in aid of certain chosen candidates. The "popular democracies" (which is of course a tautology) of the Marxist kind claim to have overcome formal democracy, but no one has yet found a way in which all the people should really govern their own state.

Throughout the New Testament it is clear that the Church founded by Jesus comes from above and is given its commission in advance. It is described in Apoc. 21. 2 as "a new Jerusalem of God coming down from heaven". Paul, in Eph. 4. 1–16, stresses that the Church exists before its members, having been founded by God's plan.

In the gospel parables, the Church is compared to a seed which grows, but the sower is always Christ or God. And there is another important consideration. A democracy does not only get its power from the people but also implies that the people really "rule". The community founded by Jesus is not a system of government (see Luke 22. 24–26).

This new dialectic was difficult to maintain, especially because the "Kingdom of God" expected by the Jews was thought of as a concrete human society. How else could the Jews have imagined various communities in which there would naturally have been different talents and functions without supposing that this would involve a form of "government", however minimal? The New Testament, however, leaves us in no doubt. Precisely because Jesus did not found a "democratic" community, we cannot hold that anyone in it—anyone at all—could claim to exercise "power". Saying that the community founded by Jesus was not democratic implies, at the very least, that, in the Church as a human community, there is no "power", not even vested in those whom God has chiefly chosen, those at the "bottom" of the community, the ordinary people, or even less, of course, in those at the "top". This is why the New Testament stresses so often the "ministerial" or serving nature of the functions exercised by those who might appear to be at the "top" of the community.

The denial of democracy to the community rests on the absolute lordship of Christ who is the only one really above all the members of the community. The distance between Christ and each member of the community is the same; no one can claim to be nearer the Lord because of his function in the Church: "To sit at my right hand and at my left is not mine to grant, but it is for those for whom it has been prepared by my Father" (Mt. 20. 23).

This is the paradox, that the non-democratic Church means precisely the people's Church. In the Church no one has power, not even the "people". All are equally under the one Lord. This means that anyone who "presides" must think of himself as a "servant" of the others, and moreover, dependent on them. A Church whose "leaders" claimed to exercise their functions independently of the people is certainly not the Church Jesus wanted and Paul described in such detail. And let it not be said that this would give rise to the danger of "demagogy"; demagogy of course means precisely the opposite, the desire to "lead" the people. In the Church, leaders must in some ways let themselves be led by the people, in whose service they are. Demagogy is merely the mask of tyranny and autocracy. But in a community where by definition there is no "government" or "power" the demagogic temptation should never arise.

III. POLITICAL MOTIVATION OF THE TRIAL OF JESUS

We return now to our main point and can say that Jesus claimed to be the "Messiah" but did not claim to exercise official power in history; he offered a "human face" to the beasts of power, all kinds of power. He therefore founded a community which was to function outside the official power structures, both in its own internal organization and in its relationships with the State. It was a dialectical position bound to annoy most of the political-religious groups in the country. This is why it is impossible to identify Jesus with any of these groups.

We see Jesus both clearly standing against the Pharisees, Sadducees, Scribes or Herodians and also maintaining certain relations with them which are not always hostile. He also attracted many from the nationalist groups, including guerrilla groups, like the Zealots. According to O. Cullmann,[2] whose findings we accept, at least four of Jesus' twelve disciples were connected with the Zealots, Simon the Zealot, the two sons of Zebedee and Judas Iscariot. This is not counting the possible translation of Peter's surname Bar-Jonah as "rebel". Does this justify Cullmann's thesis that "Jesus was condemned to the cross by the Romans *as* a Zealot?" This requires a very careful reading of the passion narratives of the four evangelists, which are indeed surprisingly in agreement. First we have the condemnation of Jesus by the religious-nationalist authorities. They tried to accuse him of attacking the Temple, but they could not sustain the charge. So they were driven to extort a confession from him of his messianic claims. Jesus admitted his claims openly, but added a continuation of his preaching of his own "christology of the Son of Man", which he had clearly preached throughout his ministry.

This was followed by his trial before the Roman governor Pontius Pilate. All the evangelists agree that the nationalist

[2] *Dieu et César* (Neuchâtel, 1956), p. 11.

leaders were Jesus' accusers at the trial conducted by the occupying power. Their accusation was couched in language guaranteed to impress the representative of Rome. "We found this man perverting our nation, and forbidding us to give tribute to Caesar, and saying that he himself is Christ the king" (Luke 23. 2). Pilate asks Jesus repeatedly whether he is a king. All the evangelists report Jesus' affirmative reply. Pilate was puzzled by the situation, unprecedented in his governorship. The nationalist leaders did not usually accuse Zealots. Why then did these leaders accuse Jesus before the occupying power of claiming to be the Messiah? Mark (15. 10) makes an interesting point here: "For he perceived that it was out of envy that the chief priests had delivered him up." This is why Pilate tried hard to get out of this situation; its ins and outs were beyond his practical mind. He was glad to find a way out when he heard that Jesus was a Galilean and so under Herod's jurisdiction.

Luke clarifies an important point about the trial (23. 12). The case of Jesus was the occasion for the re-establishing of diplomatic relations between the Roman governor and the local viceroy; these relations had been officially broken off and were now renewed. In fact the rupture was purely "diplomatic", because Pilate and Herod were both part of the imperial structure. They had to put up a show of broken relations to impress the people; the case of Jesus put an end to this hypocrisy. Jesus united the official enemies, because they were both threatened by him. The nationalist forces existed to overthrow the forces of occupation. These same nationalist forces were, throughout the gospel narratives, Jesus' main opponents. Jesus undeniably sympathized with the Zealots but did not agree with them in their fundamental desire of overthrowing the occupying power by force, because he believed that the nationalists were even more corrupt than the Romans.

The pardon of Barabbas confirms this reading of the trial of Jesus. Pilate is "testing" the chief priests and their response confirms his suspicions. Jesus was not a Zealot because then they would have treated him like Barabbas and even preferred him to Barabbas. After the "test" Pilate found a practical solution to the conflict. He wanted to please both the chief priests and the people who were their tools, and also to send a favourable dossier to

Rome to justify his actions before Caesar. He did not condemn Jesus as a "Zealot" or a "Messiah". He simply let things take their course and thus killed two birds with one stone. He pleased the Jews and justified himself before Caesar by giving him to understand that he had brought Israel under such splendid control that its own chiefs now delivered up guerrilla leaders whom they formerly protected. Thus Jesus was certainly condemned for political motives, but not precisely because he claimed to want to overthrow the reigning power, rather because his critical attitude to all power made him an insupportable nuisance to all those in power.

IV. POLITICAL COMMITMENT OF THE CHRISTIAN COMMUNITIES

The political ecclesiology of the New Testament is a complete parallel to the political christology we have outlined above. The Christian communities adopted an attitude towards authority which was a dialectic between submission and independence. The Church did not claim to take over the functions of the State, such as bearing the sword, collecting taxes and punishing criminals, but conscientiously submitted to its rule in these matters (Rom. 13. 5). But it also believed it had sole charge of the mission it had received from Christ. The *kerygma* can only be preached by the Church, because its authority goes back to Christ. This kerygmatic independence means that the Church felt able to criticize freely the actions of the State.

The above remarks can give us certain pointers about the behaviour of Christians precisely as Christians in their political compromise: (1) The political attitude of Jesus and the early Christian communities was inseparable from their proclamation of the Kingdom of God. Thus the political commitment of the Christian cannot be watered down into a purely humanitarian, progressive or revolutionary movement. It is a specifically *religious* movement. (2) The christology and the corresponding ecclesiology of the "Son of Man" implies the absolute renunciation of the exercise of temporal power. Christian communities *as such* must therefore be free from all earthly power. Christian communities must observe these two conditions in order to be able to make an effective attack on powers that exploit or oppress. This is why such "powers" are always anxious (1) to find Christians lukewarm in their religion and (2) to be able to involve Christians in their own policies of exploitation and oppression. Good revolutionary strategy should obey the maxim that one should always do the opposite of what the enemy expects.

Translated by Dinah Livingstone

Theodore Steeman

Political Relevance of the Christian Community between Integralism and Critical Commitment

I

THE problem we have to address ourselves to in this article is basically that of the social and ecclesiastical structuring of the political involvement of the Christian community. The question has been raised whether this new orientation of the Church to be concerned about the problems of society, as formulated by the Second Vatican Council and later papal documents and as propounded in the so-called political theology,[1] does not in fact lead to a new kind of integralism. This would mean that ecclesiastical power and authority are used to promote Christian involvement in the battle for justice and peace and that the same ecclesiastical structure which at earlier stages in history backed up the *status quo* now moves to a more critical approach to society.

The question goes even deeper. It is feared that efforts to organize the Christian community behind a programme of social criticism and action will increase rather than decrease the exercise of authority of the ecclesiastical power structure. Integralism, it should be noted, placed all decisions about the political behaviour of the Christian in the hierarchy, and it was a victory for the layman when he found recognition of his rightful autonomy in the political sphere. Now, with the Church entering the political arena, is this not a return to that kind of in-

[1] The most important statement is by J. B. Metz, *Theology of World* (New York, 1969).

tegralism which robs the individual Christian of his own personal responsibility in matters political? Is not a leftist integralism introduced after a rightist integralism has been successfully overcome?

There is another way in which we can formulate the problem. The socially aware Christian who moves towards radical criticism of society on the basis of his Christian convictions tends to become very critical also of those professed Christians who do not share his views or join in his actions. When convictions about social and political issues are made into religious convictions is there not the danger that a climate of intolerance will pervade the Christian community? This would be but another form of integralism. Not so much the authority structure of the Church but social pressure would endanger the legitimate autonomy of the individual Christian to form his political opinions. In this perspective it would be better if the Church or the Christian community would leave the political sphere to the individual Christian rather than making it into an area of ecclesiastical concern.[2]

Now it is, of course, far too late to argue that the problems of the modern world—war and peace, poverty, racial inequality, justice, etc.—are not a legitimate concern for the Christian conscience and Christian community, or that the Christian conscience and politics have nothing to do with each other. But the questions raised in the foregoing paragraphs are serious ones. How can this political orientation be structured in such a way as to not violate the individual freedom of the Christian? Is any development of a new integralism to be expected?

II

Let me first point out that we are dealing here with the problem of the internal structuring of the Church in view of its changing attitude *ad extra*. The concerns about the danger of integralism and intolerance, about hierarchical presumption and the rights of the layman have to do with the internal structure of the Church, whereas the political and critical engagement in the

[2] These objections are most clearly voiced by H. Maier, "Politische Theologie?", in H. Peukert (ed.), *Diskussion zur "politischen Theologie"* (Mainz, 1969), pp. 1–25.

problems of society is clearly a matter of the relation between Church and World. This distinction between the Church *ad intra* and the Church *ad extra* was made by Cardinal Suenens at the Second Vatican Council, but, however convenient the distinction may be, it should not lead us to believe that the two areas can be separated. Can one expect the Church to change its position vis-à-vis the world without feeling the repercussions of that change in its own internal structures?[3] The question we are to discuss in this article is not simply a matter of how to structure the Church, but of how to structure it in view of the new social awareness. The political involvement of the Church creates this problem.

While it is in principle not impossible that a whole national hierarchy or an individual bishop or even the Pope himself would become critically involved in the problems of modern society— one can certainly not say that *Populorum Progressio* and *Octogesima Adveniens* are uncritical documents, and, to mention only one example, some of the actions of the hierarchy in Paraguay seem to be very critical of the government—the question is whether this constitutes more than just the beginning of a real socio-critical and political involvement of the Christian community. *Octogesima Adveniens* ends with a rather passionate plea for action, an appeal more specifically to the laity, "without waiting passively for orders and directives, to take their initiative freely and to infuse a Christian spirit into the mentality, customs, laws and structures of the community in which they live".[4] It is at the level of the laity in the local Christian community, apparently, that the socio-critical involvement is to be located, that social programmes can be put into action. This prominence given to the laity should have some structural consequences.

III

Before looking into these structural consequences a few words should be said about the "Christian community" as we use the term here. The term is, on the one hand, inclusive in the sense

---

[3] Cf. Th. M. Steeman, *Conflict in the Conciliar Church*, I-DOC (Rome, 1967).
[4] *Octogesima Adveniens*, letter of Pope Paul VI to Cardinal Roy, 14 May 1971, n. 48.

that it includes all those who identify themselves as Christians and share this commitment with fellow Christians, and, on the other hand, pre-structural: it does not identify the community with the institutional Church or any kind of structure. It is typically a term which tries to avoid the lay-clergy-hierarchy conception of the Church in that it emphasizes the community aspect rather than the institutional aspect of the Church. It leaves, therefore, the question of internal structure open.

Positively speaking, the most important aspect of this Christian community for the present discussion is that it is a community in which the Christian self-awareness and self-identity and the Christian conscience are fostered. The Christian community is a community in which not only the mighty deeds of God, more specifically the life, death and resurrection of Jesus, are commemorated and celebrated, but which constitutes a community of moral discourse. It is in the community, in the conversation with his fellow Christians, that the Christian is made aware of his moral obligations, of his mission to society, of the proper understanding of the Christian presence in the world. This is important to realize: when we talk about integralism as a social pressure, it should be remembered that for the Christian the formative influence of the Christian community on the formation of his conscience is essential. There is no such thing as an individual Christian if that term would mean a Christian who does not hold himself accountable for his opinions and actions to the community of Christians. I am not talking now about the teaching authority of the Church but about the willingness of the Christian to be accountable to his fellow Christians—under the Gospel which is the ultimate norm we all have to live and to judge by. And this willingness can be expected of every Christian, wherever he may be located in the organized structure.

Now, we can say that at the present time part of the moral consciousness of the Christian community is that the Christian message means an active concern for the world, for the problems of society. We are told so not only by the Pope or by the Vatican Council, i.e., the world's bishops, but the awareness is widespread throughout the Christian community. Thus there is a sense in which a political theology is unavoidable: it articulates deeply the mind of the Christian community. And there is a sense in which this awareness of having to be as Christians concerned about such political matters as war and peace, justice, poverty, racial and sexual equality, etc., imposes itself on the Christian conscience: the Christian community as a whole has defined itself in this direction. If this be integralism, so be it. Denying this part of the Christian conscience now is equivalent to saying that a Christian in conscience could still be in favour of slavery. The individual Christian, to sum it up, is not completely free vis-à-vis the consensus of the Christian community.

IV

It is a different matter when we start looking at the way this political involvement can be structured in the Christian community. We do not need to belabour here that the traditional structure of the Catholic Church was characterized by a strong centralization of decision making and authority. Integralism was the extreme statement of this centralization: it located the power to decide about what is properly Christian in all realms of life, including the political realm, exclusively in the hierarchical structure.[5] The layman was seen as at the receiving end without any contribution of his own. Now, this kind of structure may have worked as long as the function of the Church was seen as only mediating to the layman God's grace and God's truth, as only having to do with the layman's private religious life. I am not saying that the model is beyond theological criticism; it certainly is not. I am only saying that it may have worked. We have no space here to discuss the theological merits and drawbacks of that type of structure. The point is that we have all sorts of reasons to believe that it cannot work any more, and most certainly not in a Christian community which is politically involved in society.

First of all, this socio-critical involvement creates a situation in which the Christian community enters into a dialogue with its social environment. It reacts to the social situation in function of its own moral and social awareness, but the social environment is a formative power in shaping that awareness. It is the social

[5] For a short discussion of the phenomenon of Integralism see W. Molinski, "Integralism", in *Sacramentum Mundi* III (London and New York, 1969), pp. 151–152.

fact of poverty or racial inequality that summons the Christian conscience. That is: the Christian community is not simply engaged in spelling out the socio-critical implications of its own faith, but does so in confrontation with a given world which in specific ways is not acceptable to the Christian. It is not the Church which determines what the problems of the world are; it is the world in its factuality which presents itself to the Christian community as a problem. In more technical terms we can say that non-theological data[6] becomes decisive in shaping the mind of the Christian community. This means that the Christian community in its political involvement defines itself as open to the world and as willing to shape itself in such a way as to be able to serve the world. This is clearly the opposite of integralism, which would make an unchanging Church with a fixed socio-political programme the central Christian concern.

Secondly, since the Christian community is confronted with different social problem situations on the local level—different in Latin America than in the United States, different again in Japan than in the communist world[7]—the concrete content of the Christian social awareness may vary considerably. No central authority can decide what exactly the Christian's responsibility is in a specific political situation. No general rules can be established which would apply in every case. Rather the Christian conscience is shaped in the concrete situation, in the concrete involvement in a particular society, and what is proper to do in one situation may be improper in another. This is not to deny that there should be something recognizably Christian in all these different concrete social positions. It should be possible for one Christian community to explain to another why it takes the position it is actually taking and to account for it in terms of the Gospel. This, I would think, is what constitutes the unity of the Christian Church beyond the local churches: this possibility of testifying to each other of the faith that is at work in their particular involvement in society. But the point is that the real hard decisions about socio-

[6] This point has been especially emphasized by E. Schillebeeckx, "The Magisterium and the World of Politics", in *Concilium*, June 1968 (American Edn., vol. 36).

[7] See H. Cox (ed.), *The Church Amid Revolution* (New York, 1967). Several of the articles deal with different national situations and clarify the point that the Christian conscience is faced with a variety of problems.

critical involvement have to be made in the concrete situation, not by a centralized authority.

This leads us to a third point. Moving the locus of the decision making to the concrete situation evidently means introducing a larger input of the lower levels of the Church's organization into the theological and socio-critical awareness of the Church at large. This is what I mentioned earlier: special prominence is given to the layman. We have no space here to discuss the problem—and it is a problem—of the lay-clergy-hierarchy division in the Church. Let me say that I would tend to look at the higher levels of the Church's organizational structure in terms of socio-religious leadership rather than in terms of a sacral priesthood.[8] This seems to make much more sense in the context of the conception of the Church which arose at Vatican II, and certainly in the context of a Christian community which functions as a community of moral discourse. The prominence now given to the layman in the socio-critical or political involvement of the Christian community in society would then mean that the leadership in the Church, whether lay or clerical, becomes much more dependent on the lower echelons both in terms of information and of decision making than an integralist model for Church organization could allow for. Socio-critical involvement can be encouraged from on high; it cannot be imposed and certainly not concretely defined.

There is one final consideration that should be mentioned. We have emphasized that the consensus of the Christian community limits the freedom of the individual Christian. We should add here that real consensus about positive programmes of socio-critical involvement of the Christian community may be difficult to reach. It is much easier to reach a consensus about what is wrong than about what to do about it.[9] This points to the likely persistence of a pluralism within the Christian community, to the availability of a variety of choices as far as positive action is concerned. This pluralism was recognized by *Pope Paul VI* when he stated in *Octogesima Adveniens* that "the same Christian faith

---

[8] See Th. M. Steeman, "The Priest as Socio-Religious Leader", in *Clergy in Church and Society* (Actes de la IX Conférence Internationale de Sociologie Religieuse, Rome, 1967), pp. 153–86.

[9] This point, again, was made by E. Schillebeeckx, *op. cit.*

can lead to different commitments".[10] Within the same social problem situation one may differ from his fellow Christian about the desirable course of action. Depending on where they find themselves in the concrete social situation, Christians, as all people, will probably differ in the way they analyse it and in the way they determine the right means to achieve a social objective. This is a pluralism, inherent in the situation of political involvement, which bars an integralist approach to actual programmes of action.

V

Thus we are led to conclude that the new political theology does not entail the danger of a new integralism. Basically what the argument comes down to is that the programme of political theology implies a change in the structure of the Church, away from authoritarianism and towards a greater emphasis on the Church as a community of concern. We have indicated that it also implies a restructuring of the lay-clergy-hierarchy division. And it is, I think, the fact that especially the latter pattern of change was overlooked which explains that a fear of a new integralism could arise. But when one reads, for example, J. B. Metz's work on political theology one cannot but note that implicit in that theology there is a concept of the Church which is vastly different from the traditional concept, taken in extreme terms by integralism, with its strong emphasis on the sacerdotal-hierarchical structure. It is a Church which defines itself primarily as a community of service, a Church which is willing to be critical not only of society but of itself, a Church, in short, that is less interested in itself than in what it can do for God's world. Space, however, does not allow us to pursue this topic any further. I would just like to make one more comment, namely that the restructuring of the Church we have talked about can come as a consequence of the acceptance by the Christian community of its social responsibility. Intra-Church reform as we see it is not separable from the redefinition of its goals as is done by political theology. That Church reform need not be a matter of wishful thinking. It is, rather, a matter of taking the mission of the Church to the world seriously.

[10] *Octogesima Adveniens*, n. 50.

Edward Schillebeeckx

Critical Theories and Christian Political Commitment

THE questions that I have to try to answer in this article are these. Have the contemporary emancipation movements had any influence on the critical attitude of Christian communities? What impulses can possibly emanate from the so-called critical theories and what effects do they have on praxis in the community? Finally, are there any limits to this?[1]

I. EMANCIPATION MOVEMENTS AND CRITICAL THEORIES

1. Under Roman law, man's legal status in the establishment was either that of mancipation, in which case he was made a slave by the symbolic act of "taking by the hand", or that of manumission, when he was freed from slavery, or symbolically "sent from the hand" of his master. In the Enlightenment, this emancipation was based on man's courage to "use his intellect without the guidance of others" and the emancipated, free man was one who "uses his intellect publicly at all times".[2]

We have in recent years become aware of the possible obstruction of the hermeneutical process and of mutual understanding among people by the structures of society, giving rise to a political dimension in the process of discovering the truth. What is

[1] These questions have been prompted by my recent article on "Kritische theorie en theologische hermeneutiek", in *Geloofsverstaan: Interpretatie en kritiek* (Bloemendaal, 1972), pp. 186–216.
[2] I. Kant, "Was ist Aufklärung?", W. Weischedel, ed., *Werke*, vol. 9 (Darmstadt, 1968), p. 53; W. Oelmüller, *Die unbefriedigte Aufklärung* (Frankfurt, 1969); idem, *Was ist heute Aufklärung?* (Düsseldorf, 1972).

48

more, the need to change structures that have become repressive has similarly become an essential aspect of the process of universal understanding and a prerequisite for mutual agreement among men.

One of the most important consequences of this movement of emancipation, which began with the Enlightenment and has continued unabated ever since, has been that authority together with all traditions, institutions and norms can no longer be justified simply by the fact that these already exist in society. They can only be justified in the light of human reason. Enlightened reason has become the principle of non-violent, free communication, which rejects everything that is repressive or oppressive in society and provides the means of solving all human conflicts and contradictions. The Enlightenment initiated the modern movement of emancipation, with the criticism of established religion, the abolition of slavery, the creation of parliamentary government and the struggle for civil rights in the West. What is more, the Christian critical faculty was developed not directly from the Bible or theology, but indirectly, via human reasoning.

2. In the past decade, our attitude towards this movement of emancipation which was initiated by the Enlightenment has undergone a certain change. We recognize, for example, that, during the Enlightenment, the tendency towards freedom was subject to different historical conditions from those prevailing today. In the past, God was held responsible for the evil conditions in the world that he ruled in his providence. This earlier theodicy ("justice of God") has now been replaced, since, with the Enlightenment, man has come to be regarded as the subject and the producer of his own history, by an "anthropodicy" ("justice of man"), a concrete criticism of man in society.

The advocates of these modern critical theories are without any doubt following closely the tradition of the movement towards freedom that began with the Enlightenment. They approach it, however, as twentieth-century liberals or socialists and above all as men liberated from the tutelage of religion. The most important of these critical theories relating to the movement of "emancipative freedom" have been elaborated by Ernst Bloch, who has criticized socialism for having neglected the "warm current"—the utopia—of Marxism, Herbert Marcuse, who has accused modern society of being "one-dimensional", and the members of the so-called Frankfurt school, Max Horkheimer, Theodor Adorno and Jürgen Habermas.

Following the rational principle of the Enlightenment, the industrial countries of the West have developed science and technology to the point where they have become indispensable factors in the process of emancipation. The originators of the contemporary critical theories, analysing the positivist assumptions underlying modern society with the conscious aim of furthering this process, have exposed certain alarming side-effects resulting from the "one-way traffic" of a society so firmly based on science and technology. One obvious result is that there is no possibility of an alternative way of life, nor is there much chance that true humanity or what Kant called the "good life" will survive. As Adorno has said, "the consequence of the rational and systematic control by industrial society of man's whole being, even his inner being, is that it is not really possible for any man in the modern world to live according to his own decisions".[3]

This tendency in industrial society has caused the emancipation movement of the Enlightenment to peter out and concern on the part of very many members of society for the welfare of all men to dwindle away. Almost all decisions concerning society are now in the hands of a few technocrats or politicians, usually in sharp competition with each other for ultimate control, while most people remain silent and indifferent. The main concern is that the social system should function more and more perfectly in all its sub-divisions, while questions such as "why?" or "where is it leading" are lost in the shadows. We are constantly confronted with the image of "a comfortable, smooth, reasonable, democratic unfreedom",[4] an anonymous compulsion of which many people are barely conscious.

It cannot be denied that Christians who are attempting to adapt the Church to a modern society which they have not yet subjected to critical scrutiny have much to learn from these critical theories, which have brought to light so many new forms of inhumanity caused by the present social system. The Church should above all pay attention to the just criticism that these un-

[3] T. W. Adorno, *Erziehung zur Mündigkeit* (Frankfurt, 1970), p. 151.
[4] H. Marcuse, *One-Dimensional Man* (London, 1964), p. 1.

critical attempts are in fact a legitimation of the *status quo* in society.

It is also remarkable how many of these originators of critical theories have come from Judaism and are therefore in the now secularized prophetic and critical tradition of the Old Testament and of the hope of the coming of a new, free, humane and just Kingdom of God. Even those who are not themselves Jews are influenced by the Jewish leaders of the movement, Horkheimer, Adorno and Bloch. What is more, the original "emancipative" inspiration of the Enlightenment is clearly reflected in a new form in this modern movement.

Marcuse, for example, cannot find any meaningful way out of the inner contradictions inherent in modern society. The will to renew society must come from inwardly renewed man, but a vicious circle exists because certain outward factors which are favourable to the renewal of society are also necessary for this inner renewal.[5] The only meaningful action that is possible in such circumstances is the "great refusal". This includes, on the one hand, a utopian element, a refusal to forget that it could be different, and, on the other hand, an aspect of contestation, a refusal to join in the game and a permanent criticism of the established order.[6]

Habermas is clearly dissatisfied with the model of interpretation used, not only by Marcuse, but also by Marx and Max Weber and has insisted that the concrete form of modern society is determined by the relationship between work or technical interest and communicative action or hermeneutical interest. In modern capitalist society, there is a constant danger that rational, systematic action—what Horkheimer has called "instrumental thought"—will become completely autonomous and that society will be disposed of in a purely material way, becoming a self-regulating system governed by the new "substitute ideology" of technocracy.[7] Emancipation from nature is obstructed by this process and nature itself is excessively exploited with a resulting

---

[5] *Idem, Das Ende der Utopie* (Berlin, 1967), pp. 40–1.
[6] *Idem, Triebstruktur und Gesellschaft* (Frankfurt, 1965), p. 148.
[7] J. Habermas, *Technik und Wissenschaft als "Ideologie"* (Frankfurt, 1968); *Erkenntnis und Interesse* (Frankfurt, 1968); *Zur Logik der Sozialwissenschaften* (Tübingen, 1967); *Theorie und Praxis* (Neuwied, 3rd edn., 1969); *Strukturwandel in der Öffentlichkeit* (Neuwied, 4th edn., 1969).

disturbance in man's environment. It also causes a disruption of communication between men and this in turn gives rise to repression and oppression in society. On the basis of this progressively rational and systematic activity, there is an increasing danger that man himself will become a piece of "manipulable technique".

Habermas believes that these side-effects of the emancipation movement that had its origin in the Enlightenment principle of rationality can only be overcome if we return to the fundamental inspiration of the Enlightenment itself. "The basis of the Enlightenment", he has asserted, "is that science is bound to the principle that all discussion must be free from established power structures and to no other principle."[8] This is why he is convinced that there can be only one way of achieving in complete freedom a "universal consensus" about what is true and good for man, and that is by theoretically anticipating an "ideal" situation in which dialogue is mature and free from coercion.[9]

Habermas' critical theory is indissolubly linked with a "revolutionary praxis", but he takes care to make a distinction between theory and praxis here: "The consequence of the systematic unity of theory and praxis is not a unity of scientific analysis and direct preparation for political action. This is why an appeal to the unity of theory and praxis cannot form the basis of a demand for an institutional unity of science and preparation for action. It is necessary to separate both spheres. . . . Between science and planning for action are structural differences, which call for a clear institutional division between the two. If they are identified, both are harmed—science is corrupted under the pressure of praxis and political action is led astray by a pseudo-scientific alibi."[10] This is one of the reasons why the "New Left" in Germany dissociated itself from Habermas and it is a clear indication of a loss of solidarity among the members of the so-called "Frankfurt school".

[8] J. Habermas, *Protestbewegung und Hochschulreformen* (Frankfurt, 1969), p. 245.
[9] See the controversy between H. G. Gadamer and J. Habermas in *Hermeneutik und Ideologiekritik* (Frankfurt, 1971), especially pp. 57–82.
[10] See J. Habermas, *Protestbewegung und Hochschulreformen, op. cit.*, pp. 246 and 248.

II. HAVE THESE CRITICAL THEORIES INFLUENCED THE POLITICALLY COMMITTED "CRITICAL COMMUNITIES"?

To my knowledge, there is no reference at all to these critical theories in Dorothee Sölle's "political evening prayer" at Cologne, which is the document of one of the most outstanding politically committed "critical communities" of our times.[11] This shows, I think, how careful one has to be not to speak too soon of a direct influence of these critical theories on critical Christian communities. During a four-month lecture tour of American universities early in 1971, when I came into contact with many critical groups of politically committed Christian students, I met no one who had even heard of Habermas.[12] What is more, it was only among similar students at Berkeley in California that the Frankfurt school was known and then only indirectly.[13] There were, however, active groups and a professor, who had participated in the ecumenical celebration during the student uprising in Paris in May 1968, told me that, apart from two leaders of the uprising, none of the politically committed students had at that time read any of the critical theories, although most of them had heard of the theories of Marcuse. Finally, it is certain that politically committed parishes, like Don Mazzi's in Isolotto, have no direct or indirect relations with any critical theories.

What is quite clear, however, is that, partly because of the influence of the speed of modern information services, which expose abuses in any part of the world to people everywhere, the spirit of contestation has become very widespread in recent years. We have become very conscious of the contrasts in world society —between groups in our own countries and between the prosperous and the underdeveloped countries. There have also been popular scientific prognoses concerning the year 2000 and the urgent need to take counter-measures now to avert disaster. Finally, there is a general anti-institutional and anti-ideological feeling resulting from a meaningless suffering imposed by

[11] See D. Sölle and F. Steffensky, eds., *Politisches Nachtgebet in Köln*, 2 vols. (Stuttgart, 1970–1971); *id., Politische Theologie* (Berlin, 1971).

[12] As far as I know, Habermas was first introduced to American Christians in the theological journal *Continuum* in 1971.

[13] Despite the fact that many members of this school found refuge in the United States during the Nazi regime.

bureaucracy. All these phenomena have given rise to a widespread malaise in society, a malaise made more acute by the fact that so many young people—"hippies" and others—have opted out of a society that seems to them to be meaningless.

Signs of a "counter-culture" and a "new consciousness", an "anti-history" existing alongside the "official" history, indicate clearly enough that our society has in a sense reached a dead end. Criticism of this society in a spirit of sharp contestation has led to the development, at the level of systematic thought, of critical theories and, at the level of Christian praxis, of politically committed critical communities.

Whereas the Church has, until quite recently, been judged only according to evangelical or theological criteria, it has now come to be regarded as one part of the whole complex establishment of society and as such subject to the same criticism as such institutions as parliament, the legal system, state education, and so on, all of which share in the evils of society. All these structures are so closely interrelated that, in remaining aloof from political contestation, especially in the case of any struggle between those in power and the "poor", is in fact a pronounced favouring of those in power. It is above all this situation which has made many Christian communities critical not only of society as a whole, but of the institutional Church in particular. To regard this as an infiltration of un-Christian, even demonic elements into the Church is to be blind to the "signs of the times" and is attributable to a false ideology or to wrong information.

The specifically Christian aspect of this criticism of the Church and society comes from a new understanding of Jesus of Nazareth and the Kingdom of God, often stimulated by study at various levels. Although some recent popular works have provided an exaggerated and historically distorted picture of Jesus as a revolutionary engaged in political contestation, others are exegetically more sound in their presentation of the political relevance of the appearance of Jesus as a political figure.[14]

Because of the present historical situation and a new under-

---

[14] See, for example, R. Pesch, *Von der "Praxis des Himmels"* (Graz, 1971); O. Cullmann, *Jesus und die Revolutionären seiner Zeit* (Tübingen, 1970); H. W. Bartsch, *Jesus. Prophet und Messias aus Galiläa* (Frankfurt, 1970).

standing of the historical Jesus, these critical communities on the one hand long for freedom, humanity, peace and justice in society and, on the other, resist the power structures that threaten these values by repression or oppression. What J. Jüngel has called "a Kingdom of God mindful of humanity", a rule that has been handed down to us in the tradition of the Old and New Testaments, inevitably makes Christians feel at one with the contemporary emancipation movements, although they have a critical attitude towards their violent and one-sided tendencies and subject them to the criterion of the "life praxis of Jesus".

It would be quite wrong to accuse these Christian critical communities of being inspired by Marxist infiltrators, above all because there is so much Marxist criticism of the Marxist system and because there are social evils in Marxist communist societies just as there are under capitalism. What Christian critical communities have derived from Marxism are very valuable aids to the analysis of society. The Marxist system, however, is subjected to sharp criticism. It cannot, of course, be denied that there are Marxist-Christian student cells in many countries. It would, however, be a mistake to think that all student and other communities are of this kind and, especially in the case of Latin America, where all freedom movements are labelled as communist, it is important to take this idea of Marxist infiltration with a grain of salt.

III. Christian Limits and Corrections

1. In contemporary society, it is impossible to believe in a Christianity that is not at one with the movement to emancipate mankind. The reverse is also true—Christianity has also become incredible to those who, against all Christian reason, persist in maintaining their established positions in society. This is a distinctively modern form of the stumbling-block of Christian faith, the direct cause of which is not Christianity itself, but the evidance of these privileged positions of power that are accepted without question.

If this Christian solidarity with the modern critical emancipation movements is not to produce a replica of what is being done elsewhere in the world by Christians simply as men and by many others, then the Christian promise that inspires this solidarity has to be expressed and celebrated. The Church is, after all, the community of God called out by Jesus Christ and its message is both promise and criticism—criticism and political commitment on the basis of God's promise in Jesus Christ.

The question that arises in this context is this—is the freedom which these emancipation movements are seeking a utopian ideal without a definite direction, postulated as correlative with the contrasts in the world? Is there any basis for any definite expectation? We have seen that Marcuse was unable to answer this question and continues to believe in a utopia that cannot be realized and that Habermas believes in an ideal community in which dialogue is free from coercion as the norm for all attempts at emancipation.

How, then, can this postulate be justified and can the dialectical tension between "institution" and "freedom" ever be resolved? Is it perhaps not true to say that being man is simply a permanent attempt to become free within this tension? The expectation of a utopia that can never be realized rules out the possibility of provisional theoretical and practical solutions. It always contains the threat of totalitarianism, of a betrayal of the truly human quest for freedom, of an ultimate withdrawal from the struggle because of impotence with regard to the provisional renewal of society or even of a final resorting to violence.

This belief in a utopia is also based on the assumption that man's release from institutional structures will automatically bring about more freedom and humanity. "Radical negativity", however, may cause more unfreedom and inhumanity than the structures of society. Man can never be completely identified with his own products—either his good structures or his bad ones. Marcuse has drawn attention to a vicious circle in the dialectical tension between the need for man to find a "new heart" and the necessity for good structures which make him free but at the same time "institutionalize" freedom itself.

The Christian community therefore has the task of considering whether faith in the redemption, with its negative aspect of original sin, can provide a perspective which will have the effect of bringing freedom here and now in the light of the Christian promise. During a congress at Nijmegen University, L. Kolakowski, who is clearly disillusioned with all systems, declared that he does not expect Christians to do what Marxists have already done better, but hoped that they would let the special contribution of the Christian tradition be heard. (I would add that they should do this in conjunction with what the Marxists have done.) Kolakowski was thinking especially of the Christian doctrine of original sin in this context, not of the positive doctrine of redemption.

It is possible for a critical community to be politically committed, but to fail to provide this distinctively Christian perspective and to celebrate the promise in the liturgical language which prayerfully expresses the transcendent element. Such a community might achieve very fruitful results, but it would not be acting as a Christian community. It would be in danger of becoming a purely political cell without evangelical inspiration—one of very many useful and indeed necessary political pressure groups, but not an *ecclesia Christi*.

2. Elsewhere, Kolakowski has said that, in order to solve the conflicts in human history, man has to depend on an arsenal of means "which can only be found in human traditions".[15] Paul Ricoeur too has often drawn attention to the fruitful practice of critically remembering human traditions in a society such as ours, which has lost its historical roots and has come to depend on scientific planning and prognosis of the future. A true revival of the principle of the Enlightenment cannot take place either by rejecting all traditions or by making them all hermeneutically present. It can only be done by a critical remembrance of certain traditions. It was precisely in this way that the Western movement of emancipative freedom came about. We internalize the past not in order to make it present here and now, but rather to save for the future certain values which might otherwise have been lost in the past. An option for the future thus always mediates the critical remembrance of the past. This remembrance therefore is an eminent factor in the human process achieving freedom, which in turn always tends to be one-dimensional.

The Christian memory contains much more, of course, than a concrete remembrance of "critical theories", which is basically

[15] L. Kolakowski, "Der Anspruch auf die selbstverschuldete Mündigkeit", in L. Reinisch, ed., *Vom Sinn der Tradition* (Munich, 1970), p. 3.

no more than a recollection of rationality as the Enlightenment principle of freedom. Generally speaking, as Habermas has pointed out, our critical remembrance of the traditions of the great religions of the world is of great importance in the process of achieving freedom and in the search for a truly human identity.[16] In this, we are faced with the irreducible contribution made by the non-scientific freedom movements, which in many respects go further than the rational principle of the Enlightenment on which all the modern critical theories are based. These non-scientific religious traditions provide the concept of "emancipation", which is in itself abstract, utopian and without content, with a very concrete content, which is in turn able to give a positive orientation to the movement of emancipative freedom, not, however, without the mediation of human reason, which is both analytical and interpretative.

Within this remembrance of varied religious inspiration, Christians find, in the life praxis of Jesus, that is, in their remembrance of his life and of his death and resurrection, both the basis of the promise and the criticism which comes from this and at the same time an orientation for their action in making the world free.[17] Jesus the Christ is, in other words, the norm for the Christian's emancipative interest. The Christian does not regard the perspective of the Kingdom of God, of the human freedom for which he is looking, as a utopia. For him, this is something that is already given—it has already been realized in a concrete historical form in the life praxis of Jesus, whose proclamation of the Kingdom of God is the thematization of this praxis. Habermas speaks of a purely theoretical anticipation of the ideal of a "good life" lived in a community in which communication is free from coercion. The Christian, on the contrary, in his practical anticipation, follows Jesus in his activity in bringing about freedom. Jesus' motivation in this praxis of life led in the service of freedom to be found in his relationship with God, his Father, who set him free to identify himself with all men.

The principle of rationality ultimately comes to grief because of its concept of freedom itself—even in an ideal community, we

[16] J. Habermas, *Philosophisch-politische Profile* (Frankfurt, 1971), p. 35.
[17] In addition to R. Pesch, *Von der "Praxis des Himmels"*, *op. cit.*, see also H. Kessler, *Erlösung und Befreiung* (Düsseldorf, 1972).

are confronted with the freedom of our fellow man, who may freely reject the principle that all conflicts in society can be resolved by communication which is free from coercion. This at once gives rise to a dilemma—should our fellow man, whose freedom is differently orientated, be coerced?

The Christian who remembers critically the religious traditions of mankind will know that the only justified basis for the freedom movement is a religious redemption, the freedom of God's forgiveness, which has to be given form in man's history. All Christian praxis is founded on faith in God and the critical community that does not express and celebrate this faith liturgically is cutting itself off from the source from which it draws its strength to live and work for freedom precisely as a Christian community. In that case, it may, even if its inspiration is very humane, ultimately pursue a very inhumane policy—"created in the world, five Vietnams, three Bangla Deshes and Biafras, and the system *will* collapse". Although he has lost his lustre, man still has enough humanity to be able to take that. A Christian community that is critical has, however, to be constantly alert to temptations of this kind, which sacrifice people to a better system —Max Horkheimer, for example, has spoken of man's "longing that the murderer should not triumph over the innocent victim".[18] The Christian critical community must always be conscious of the limits to man's critical reason. It should also be critical of the ideological distinction between "faith" and "religion", that is, its own religion. Finally, it should remain rationally open to the mystery of Christian life which cannot be manipulated—*intellectus quaerens fidem*. These and other conditions must be fulfilled if the Christian critical community is to be truly human and truly Christian.

3. I should like to conclude with a few words about the "deprivatization" of human subjectivity. There has been a good deal of criticism in recent years both of the privatizing tendency in the middle-class idea of man as a subject and of the opposite tendency to eliminate the subject. In this, the Christian critical community will recall the implications both of Jesus' message concerning the people of God and the Kingdom and of Jesus' life

[18] M. Horkheimer, *Die Sehnsucht nach dem ganz Anderen* (Hamburg, 1970), p. 62.

praxis as directed towards the individual. The Christian deprivatization of the subject is clearly to be found in mutual recognition
of man as a free subject situated within (changing) structures.
Without the recognition of and respect for the personal freedom
or subjectivity of the individual, criticism of social or political
action is hardly credible.

The critical community must therefore be bold enough to risk
involvement both in action to achieve freedom and to change
society and also in counselling and consoling individuals who
have got into difficulties, even if these Christian therapeutic
functions at the same time tend to justify the existing social
structures. The promise of salvation here and now extends to all
men and, even if the structures of society still cannot be made
more just, this salvation can be brought to individuals here and
now. The Christian may be committed to the task of bringing
salvation to the whole of society in the form of better and more
just structures for all men, but, until these structures have been
created, he cannot and should not, in the meantime, that is, during the whole of the eschatological interim period, overlook one
single individual fellow man. Many contemporary expressions
of Christian charity have social and political dimensions, but
inter-personal charity practised by politically committed critical
communities of Christians is still relevant and meaningful even
if it has been thrust into the background of the community's
activities.

Precisely because it claims to be Christian, no critical community can ever become an exclusive "in group" refusing mem-
bership to others who think differently. It must remain open and
reject discrimination. In the inevitable case of structural difficulties, it will always be necessary to seek provisional solutions,
which will be plausible in the Christian sense and even officially
recognized by the Church. The critical community must, moreover, never forget that, in imitation of Jesus, it is seeking freedom
not so much for itself as for others.

Jesus' apparently vain sacrifice of love arose from the contrast
between his experience of the living God and his memory of the
accumulated suffering of mankind. Yet this sacrificial death
seems to contradict the message of the Kingdom of God that
Jesus brought to man and the praxis of the life that he lived.

None the less, his death on the cross is justified by God, in the prophecy of the Christian community, concerning Jesus' resurrection, as the norm for the "good life" lived in freedom and seeking freedom for others.

Translated by David Smith

Ludwig Rütti

The Political Position of the Christian Community in the Light of "Political Theology"

THE contribution of "political theology" to an understanding of the political position of the Christian community must be more than the application to the community of a general thesis about the social mission of Christians and the Church. This would be no more than a modification of the traditional "theology of the community" which was conceived of explicitly as prior to any actual situation or practice and sets out the eternally valid characteristics and basic structures of the community. But if "political" introduces a critical and hermeneutical category into theology, this model of theological reflection is itself called in question. The mutual relations of politics, community and theology must themselves be made explicit and analysed. This article will try to relate these questions to the community as such, and in the process the idea and nature of the community will themselves inevitably be discussed and "community" will necessarily be discussed in its wider ecclesiastical and social context. I shall not discuss the political activities or politicization of individuals, groups or even communities, but the political position of the community as embodied in its understanding of itself, its structure, relation to its environment, practical organization and organizational theory.

I. THEOLOGY AND COMMUNITY

One of the main areas in which a closer connection between theory and practice has been called for in recent times is that of

theology and the shape of the community. The relationship between theory and practice referred to, however, has for the most
part been very vague and ambiguous. It was never clear in any
particular case what form of community, practice and theology,
and what theoretical and practical contexts were meant. If the
problem of theory and practice in its modern socio-political sense
is a fundamental question for theology and the Church,[1] the relationship between theology and community, with its political
implications, must be included in the question about the theological basis of the political activity of the community. Simply to call
on theologians to take an interest in the practical problems of
Church and community, or on the practical men to acquire a
grasp of theology, would be more likely to obscure the obstacles
to a transcending of the theory-practice dichotomy which are
rooted in the basic characteristics of theological theory, in its
institutional role, in ecclesiology and consequently in the "theology of the community" and in the practical organization of the
community.

The formal separation between theory and practice in the general context of theology and the Church reflects the distinction
in ecclesiology between the essence and the appearance of the
Church, which is also fundamental to the "theology of the community". The theological statements about the "essence" of the
Church are derived from the "historical revelation" found in the
Bible and the Church's dogmatic tradition, but are understood as
essential and normative statements whose status is prior to and
higher than any historical situation or manifestation. In this view
the Church appears primarily as a "supernatural essence" with
"transcendental features". This ideal transcendental essence of
the Church must become "incarnate" in historical manifestations,
subject to the limitations of space and time, in order to be present
to men, and for this reason local ties and organizational form are
essential features. "The Church—like any social group—has a
history. History is part of her essence, and this essence reveals
itself in the changing forms of her historical existence, realizes
itself in them, shows constantly different sides of the self-same

[1] Cf. J. B. Metz, *Theology of the World* (London and New York, 1969);
idem., "Political Theology", *Sacramentum Mundi*, vol. 3 (London and
New York, 1969).

ground of existence with every movement of the course of history.... This means that the basic conditions of her existence as a human community are to a large extent predetermined; they follow the lines of what is historically possible. The Church must pour her essence into these possibilities; they provide her with the clothes or, better, the body in which she reveals herself."[2] The ontology of essence and appearance which lies behind this view of Church and community leaves its mark on the whole conception. The simultaneous separation and close connection between supernatural essence and particular form of the Church on the one hand gives ecclesiastical structures and institutions the highest possible legitimation, and on the other makes possible certain changes and allows defects to appear as incomplete realizations. The social existence of the Church can be presented as "specific" and "unique" in contrast to all other "merely human" social forms, and so also, as regards the "essential", remain out of reach of sociological procedures. This ecclesiology forms a closed theory in which transcendental justification, aims, organizational structure and relation to the environment mutually reinforce each other and guarantee the identity and continuity of the social form.[3]

This model places Church and community at once in uncritical dependence on, and non-communicative isolation from, historical factors and situations. The actual development of church structures, in particular of the parish as a local community, takes place through adaptation to and adoption of existing secular social and administrative forms. But when this process is considered in the light of the "principle of the incarnation", the social structures become no more than points of attachment, a "natural basis", by means of which the Church's own form of community, which comes "from above", becomes present—always except when adaptations of administrative and pastoral methods are

[2] A. Jansen, *Die Kirche in der Grossstadt. Überlegungen zu Organisations- und Strukturfragen der Kirche in der industriellen Grossstadt* (Freiburg, 1969), p. 9.

[3] Cf. G. Bormann and S. Bormann-Heischkeil, *Theorie und Praxis kirchlicher Organisation. Ein Beitrag zum Problem der Rückständigkeit sozialer Gruppen* (Opladen, 1971). This study deals mainly with the Lutheran theology of the Church and the organization of the church in Württemberg, but the analysis holds, *mutatis mutandis*, for the Catholic Church and its communities.

concerned. In its inner essence, the Church community is first of all identical with itself and to that extent independent of historical and social conditions. In its "supernatural essence" the Church means the social and communal existence of men in exemplary form, but it is at the same time apolitical and asocial because it on the one hand manifests a social form of a higher order and on the other only takes on a concrete social form by "entering into history", into "natural" human and social conditions. The Platonic theory of the materialization of an Idea and the principle *gratia supponit naturam* seem in this view each to interpret the other. As a result, on considering the structure of the Church community neither the existing social conditions in their real complexity nor the extent to which theology and the organizational structures of the Church are themselves shaped by social and political factors are taken into account. This is prevented from the start—and this gives rise to the increasing isolation—by the transcendental justification of Church and theological knowledge and through the way of thought arising from this, which is Church-centred, based on dichotomies (Church-world, theology-secular knowledge, etc.) and claims universal validity.

An analysis employing the methods of the sociology of knowledge and the critical study of ideologies could show that this ecclesiological model and this theology church-community relation were themselves—at least in their best-known forms—determined by history. It can be shown that the opposition between a hypostatized "supernatural essence" of the Church and its concrete historical manifestation (incarnation) has as a political implication the dissolution of the unity between Church and society in the modern period. As long as the Church still had a clear function in society, there was no free-floating idea of the Church. The growth of "secularization", emancipation and the increasing complexity of society mean that the "spiritual" and the "secular" are no longer two complementary elements in a larger whole, and the changes which have made society more complex have also made the inner (hierarchical and sacral) structure of the Church more sharply distinct from general social structures. The resulting loss of the Church's social basis and visibility has produced an "abstract" idea of the Church, with "transcendental" features which now can and must be made "incarnate" in any existing social structures. Even if such a description of the Church and its essential marks is composed exclusively of medieval, patristic or New Testament ideas and images—the abstract and transcendental approach makes this easier—the "same" ideas and images have different ideological and political functions in the early Church, the Constantinian era and modern times.

In the attempt to provide a theological basis for a community's political position the relationship between theology and community must itself be regarded as a basic political problem. It would be fatal both to the community's political commitment and to theology if the ontological model and its corresponding theological methods were retained as the basis for dealing with political questions, even if they were to be treated in a utopian or progressive way. Theology's main contribution to the clarification of the political role of the Church is critical analysis and the prevention of hasty and crypto-ideological adaptations.

This fundamental questioning follows not only from political responsibility and political hermeneutics, but is also called for by the current situation of the Church and Christian groups. Social changes have brought about a crisis in the traditional ecclesiastical structures and institutions and in the ecclesiological ideas connected with them. They can no longer be taken for granted as points of departure or of reference in ecclesiological discussions or ecclesiastical reforms. This has become clear largely through the emergence of new forms of community, spontaneous and local groups. Such groups constitute a questioning in particular of the ontological model of the Church and theology. "All ecclesiological schemas are made totally relative. The creation and development of lively, flexible and provisional groups, each devised to suit its own situation, original and full of ideas and initiatives, has fallen like a whipstroke across the hierarchical, collegial, conciliar, presbyteral or synodal structures of the various Catholic, Orthodox and Protestant institutions."[4] This situation calls for a theology which is a "critical reflection on practice",[5] and also

---

[4] G. Casalis, in R. Metz and J. Schlick (ed.), *Die Spontangruppen in der Kirche* (Aschaffenburg, 1971), p. 142.

[5] Cf. G. Gutierrez, *Teología de la liberación. Perspectivas* (Lima, 1971), pp. 20–34.

raises the question of the method and subject both of the theology and the practice. If the main interest is the creation of a new form of "community", the relationship between theology and community is no longer a secondary or accidental matter, but one which determines the future course of Church and theology.

II. A Politically Active Community or a Political Community?

The justification or assessment of the community's political position must take account of the character of the community and the general relations between Church and society. In this connection we can distinguish two forms in the present situation: the local community which takes on political activity within its traditional framework and the "political community" newly created on the basis of a prior political commitment. These are not intended as two ideal or typical models capable of static description and fitting into the existing typologies of community, but two tendencies, each with its own theological, ecclesiastical and social background.

1. The Politically Active Local Community

Attempts have begun in recent times in both the Catholic and Protestant Churches to adapt traditional pastoral and community structures to social changes and to emphasize different aspects of the theology of the community. The basic premise is still that the local community, like the Church as a whole, embodies a unique social form, resulting, of course, from the transcendental origin of the Church and its inner structure. In contrast to the juridical and administrative view of the local community which predominated in the past and saw the local community as the lowest and smallest local unit in a single pastoral, administrative and legal structure, the emphasis is now on the local community's communal character and independence. The marks of the Church as a whole are also correspondingly transferred in recent theology to the local community. Even if the territorial boundaries of the community are made more fluid as a result of a redistribution of functions based on a city or a region as a whole, and as a result of the growth of "functional communities", the community still retains its primary character of a local community both in practical Church organization and in theology: the local community gives salvation specific spatial and temporal form and makes the Church present among men and in the various areas of human life.

This is the context in which the call for political commitment on the part of the community has to be understood. It is a change from a model of the community as a purely religious welfare organization directed towards the salvation of individual men understood as an individual or individualistic process to a model in which the community is "present" to all men in all their experiences and anxieties.

Various motives can be seen for this change. The Church has recognized that the traditional pastoral methods and community structures were no longer reaching large numbers of people, including many baptized Catholics, because such people felt that the Church had nothing to say to them in their problems and in many areas of their lives. People realized that the traditional community had become narrow and isolated, and that new ways of making the Church present in new environments, especially among the workers, had to be found. There was also, finally, a recognition of the social and political dimension of faith, or at least a recognition that Christians or the community (also) had a social and political responsibility. A typical feature of this form of political activity is that it is distinguished from the "true" religious mission of the Church and made subordinate to it, is based on the Church community's universal claims and remains ultimately Church-centred. These aspects are determined by the Church's relation to the society around it and consequently provide a ready-made political aspect to the existence of the community and theological study.

The process of the separation of Church and society, of civil and religious communities, leads to a loss of function or a change of function for the Church in its social context. The main feature of this is that the community's social basis, and with it many of its opportunities for contact with men, disappear. In the development of democratic societies the community becomes one element in a pluralist society, and gradually accepts this role and makes it the basis of its activity. The loss of role, narrowing of the social basis and reduction of direct contact rooted in the social system are now interpreted as the community's freedom, autonomy and distinctiveness, and also as an opportunity and obligation to become committed in as many areas as possible. "Community" comes to be seen—though not usually explicitly—as the centre of a far-reaching structure of relationships. The community's "original" autonomy and distinctiveness deriving from its transcendental origin (divine foundation, specific purpose and specific form of community) make it a fundamental starting-point for all concerns, including non-religious ones, by virtue of its "universal mission". The community appears as a subject with—at least in theory—universal responsibility, as an "absolute" subject. In fact, however, the Church community has come to an arrangement with other social and political institutions in the course of their historical confrontations; and spheres of competence have been demarcated, though it is always possible for demarcation disputes to occur. This *de facto* compromise does not, however, affect the theory of Church and community, or if it does then only in secondary questions and practical applications, because of the peculiar character of the theory, its autonomous, totalizing Church-centredness.

The community's view of itself allows it many forms of activity in the social and political field, but it is striking that the social and charitable services provided by the Christian community are almost indistinguishable from those provided by other organizations and by the public welfare services, and they create the same impression of a social apparatus. There are always gaps to be filled somewhere, there is always something to be done somewhere. This observation in no way minimizes the value of the help given and the relief provided in situations of real distress, but from the point of view of the theological and political status of this activity neither a community understood in theological terms nor any specific theological basis seem to be necessary. Indeed, they may involve the danger of a super-legitimation and ideologizing of this activity. In this context common sense and a willingness to help are enough.

On the other hand, general motivation makes willingness to help more frequent among Church people and easier to appeal to explicitly than in other social circles and bodies. As a result the community, which as such has no social function but nevertheless functions as a social institution and can in certain conditions be activated, can be mobilized for such tasks. Often, however, such socio-political activity on the part of the Christian community lacks a specifically political understanding of the relevant situation. Problems are individualized and treated as inevitable problems of fate or the social order. They stimulate no analysis of the social and political causes of such problems and no actions aimed at changing the social order which produces them. Nevertheless, a commitment to charitable work in local communities is increasingly becoming the basis for a growth in political awareness which leads to more fundamental analyses of Church and society and to a firmer political commitment. This is especially true of student groups and "critical communities". Very soon, however, such developments provoke a reaction from traditionally minded members of the community and Church leaders.

2. The Political Community

Although without more precise definition it is open to misunderstanding, the term "political community" will be used here to describe a new type of Christian community which comes into existence and organizes itself explicitly around the political implications of the relations between Church and society. Such communities take on a variety of forms according to their particular situation, interests and aims, and may be action groups, spontaneous groups, grass-roots groups or critical communities. They see themselves as Christian groups or communities, criticize the existing attitudes of the Church and Church communities and try to find new forms of community and communal commitment. They come into being through changes in existing local communities, through the division of local communities or religious communities or through new formations on a local or interregional basis. In spite of the variety of these groups and communities, some common features and tendencies can be observed under the general heading of "political position", even if not all are present to the same degree in each.

The main interest is not in the formation of a community for its own sake, but in the Gospel and Christian life in the modern world. Where, however, this commitment leads to the formation of groups and communities, these adopt forms which are in themselves a criticism, implicit or explicit, of current ecclesiastical and social structures. Their basis is personal decision, not a baptismal certificate or residence in a particular place. They try to find forms of communication in which the individual can develop fully through the group and through participation in common experiences, discussions and actions, as a contrast to the rigidly authoritarian, technocratic and anonymous procedures of ecclesiastical and social institutions. Their flexibility, deep communication and solidarity with other groups enable them to achieve an openness to world problems and a critical examination of the meaning of faith for which the only counterpart offered by official Church institutions is often only a structurally determined, and largely unsuccessful, exhortation to community as a sharing of love, to brotherliness, shared responsibility, and to carrying out the universal missionary task and the world mission.

In these communities, political criticism and political commitment cannot start from a theoretical opposition between Church and politics, Church and society, or from the allegedly apolitical character of the Church (and its traditional local communities) in its historical forms. "Political" criticism of society as a whole includes criticism of a Church which compromises with repressive and unjust social forces, and "religious" criticism of ecclesiastical mentalities and structures similarly always keeps in view their socio-political function. This is why politically committed groups concentrate on the Church's "extra-territorial" claims in social and political affairs, which remove it from the sphere of political criticism and disguise its actual political function. G. Casalis holds "that the essential feature of the spontaneous groups is to be found in those who accept the reality of politics and the risks of political action", out of which emerge the following key questions. "Are the churches willing to analyse themselves or let themselves be analysed in political terms? What position do we and they adopt in the face of the scandalous findings of these analyses, which, almost without exception, show the churches as on the side of the 'established disorder'? Are the structures of the churches politically indifferent, harmful or important? . . . Is the gospel politically neutral? If so, we must take the risk of admitting it. If not, we must have the courage to live accordingly! . . .

The essential problem for me is to find the most substantial and detailed answer possible to the double question which in my view is at the heart of the challenge presented by our time to the churches, their faith, their apostolate and their ministry of service in its individual and collective aspects: the Christian hermeneutics of politics and the political hermeneutics of Christianity."[6]

This new situation makes it impossible to avoid facing social and political conflicts; the Church community cannot escape them because they penetrate into the Church itself. In the face of this political reality, what does it mean to talk about "the unity of the Church" or "Christian brotherhood"? Talk of the "transcendental essence" and "transcendental unity" of the Church can easily create the illusion that the Church is above parties, races and the contradiction between rulers and oppressed, above the class struggle, and can have a real existence in a realm (of sermons, liturgy and sacraments) which is untouched by these fundamental political conflicts and has no effect on them. It is in the first place the Churches and communities in the rich, traditionally Christian countries, with systems still marked by the existence of a national or state Church, which must let themselves be confronted with these questions by the growing number of common-purpose and grass-roots groups in the "underdeveloped" countries, especially in Latin America, and with the "theology of liberation" which is being created in this situation, but with reference to world-wide political and ecclesiastical conditions. Political consciousness and political activity for the traditional local communities in the "developed" industrial countries would then mean in the first place becoming aware of their own position in social and international conflicts, both as regards their religious and moral attitudes, inner structures and relations with Churches in other countries, and as regards their social and charitable work at local, national and international levels.

III. The Community as a Subject of Political Action

In the process of giving a theological justification for the adoption of a political position by the community the question also

---

[6] G. Casalis, *op. cit.*, pp. 219 ff.

arises of the sense in which a community can be the subject of political action. Critical discussion and political hermeneutics of faith and the reality of the Church cannot start out unquestioningly with a reference to the transcendental origin of the Church community as a subject which must *also* be present and active in politics, since this assumption itself contains a number of political implications. Nor is the question of the subject of political action presented to the communities from outside or in purely theoretical form, but arises out of the present situation in the Church, out of the emergence of "political communities" and out of their ideas, and out of the attacks on them by other groups in the Church. All we can attempt here is to outline a few possibilities in this extremely complicated theological, ecclesiastical, social and political situation.

The general concepts of the political, of the subject of political praxis and of political institutions conceal important distinctions and varieties of political commitment which are also relevant to a theological enquiry. "Any particular concept of the political, the basic premise of political science, which gives it its basis and defines its scope, does more than determine the limits of the answers; it defines the political reality to be examined and labels particular segments of reality political or politically relevant or indifferent."[7]

This is also true of theological and ecclesiastical arguments about political responsibility. Here history must also be taken into account. Just as for political thought in general, so for "political religion", the role in which Christianity in the West replaced the Roman state religion, the realm of the political coincided with the State, with the organs and functions of the State, and with the ecclesiastical institutions which supported it. The political relevance of Christianity thus came to mean for the most part a metaphysical and religious legitimation of the existing (political) order. Then, in the wake of the Enlightenment, there arose a distinction between the state and society. Society itself became the area of political activity, in the form of the public domain in which the interests of all men as a social whole were articulated;

---

[7] W.-D. Narr, in G. Kress and D. Senghaas (ed.), *Politikwissenschaft. Eine Einführung in ihre Probleme* (Frankfurt, 1972), pp. 17 ff.

it became the area in which men's freedom was mediated and realized, the freedom of each individual and the freedom of all, in all aspects of life. This historical situation has given rise to a distinction with regard to the bearer of Christian political commitment. Where the ecclesiastical institution as one Church and as local communities still has much of the character of a state Church and so is a force in the political structure in its own right, it tends towards a theologico-political commitment on the pattern of the earlier political religions, though nowadays in different forms. "Critical communities", on the other hand, seek to encourage the political process of enlightenment and emancipation and to demolish unenlightened structures of authority and survivals of the state Church in Church and theology.

As a result, the real problem of the political position of the communities for theology and Church lies not in the acceptance or extension of political activities within the framework and under the assumptions of the traditional consciousness of the local community, but in the question how a "political community" (or the Church), which today exposes itself without reservation to the theoretical and practical challenge of politics, is to understand its Christian identity. Since the self-validation of the Church community on the ontological model (essence and appearance, incarnation of a transcendental Church subject) and the *a priori* legitimation of theologico-political statements are themselves being subjected to critical analysis as a political ideology, the question of the "transcendence", identity and uniqueness of the Church and community as subject must be formulated in a new way and in new categories. The pat criticism that the "political communities" "foreshorten" the faith and introduce a partiality which endangers the substance and the unity of the faith is based on patterns of thought which have become inadequate and cannot grasp processes of Christian practice and theological enquiry which are already under way.[8] "Is it not the distinguishing mark of this Church that it does not possess its identity in itself? That it cannot simply live from itself, from the mere reproduction of its own traditions? . . . The 'impure' relationship

[8] On this, cf. the argument between the German Catholic Students' Union (KDSE) and the German Bishops' Conference and the various positions there adopted, in *Initiative* (Bonn), 11 (1971), No. 4.

to the world is part of the definition of the Church; the Church is determined by a relationship of permanently 'unfinished business' with the world."[9]

Applied to the theoretical and practical relation of theology and Church in the present situation, this means that, in their responsibility for the eschatological and social message of Christianity, they cannot short-circuit the details of the social mediation of faith. A theological validation of the adoption of a political position by the Christian community requires first of all a new relationship between theory and practice, between theology and (basic) community. This relationship of theory and practice "will make it possible to release faith from its bonds of pure theory, and so also from the domination of the past, in order to make it free for the promised future. The absolutism of theory and the supremacy of the past go hand in hand, so that only a dialectical relationship of 'theory and practice' can unlock the future dimension."[10] Only on that condition will the promise, mission and claim of Church and community to be at the service of the salvation of all men and of the whole man avoid being invisibly perverted into an instrument of alienation and domination over men. A renewal of the preaching function and reform of the Church and its communities can only be justified if it is carried out with an awareness of politics as embracing the whole area of human life.

Translated by Francis McDonagh

[9] J. B. Metz, *Reform und Gegenreformation heute. Zwei Thesen zur ökumenischen Situation der Kirchen* (Mainz, 1969), pp. 34-5.
[10] F. van den Oudenrijn, *Kritische Theologie als Kritik der Theologie. Theorie und Praxis bei Karl Marx—Herausforderung der Theologie* (Munich, 1972), p. 20.

Norbert Greinacher

The Christian Community and Political Commitment

I. Does the Christian Community have a Political Mandate?

THE question of a political mandate for the Christian community is posed in ever-changing terms, depending upon the prevailing circumstances. But three particular situations can be distinguished. In one there is the more or less strongly Church-conscious situation found chiefly among the West European countries where in the past, and to a lesser extent in the present also, a connection exists between the Church and the political establishment, or between the Church and particular political parties. In such a situation the tendency nowadays is to dissolve this partnership of Church and State in favour of dividing the workload and keeping the Christian community quite distinct from political life.

Then there is the situation prevailing among the socialist countries of Eastern Europe in which the State ensures that the Church plays no political role whatsoever, unless it be to support the viewpoint of those in power. In these situations one can sometimes observe a remarkable unity of interest between party and Church leaders, who make common cause when it comes to nipping in the bud any ideas or movements critical of the system.

A different situation prevails in the developing countries where the chief question is what attitude the Christian community should adopt towards the national freedom movements: support for the political powers whose object is to maintain the social, economic and political *status quo*, or involvement in the revolutionary movements.

This very crude outline of the three most obvious situations at least serves to demonstrate the variety of forms in which the question of a political mandate for the Christian community can arise; it should also clearly suggest that the answer to the question necessarily depends on the particular situation.

To avoid misunderstandings, it is worth recalling what has already been said in the editorial, namely that the word "political" should be understood here in its original and widest sense and not be restricted only to the sphere of the State and its government. The word must be allowed to refer to activities within society as a whole. In this very broad sense, Jesus of Nazareth had political relevance—as elsewhere in this number González-Ruiz has sought to demonstrate. It is in this sense also that throughout history the Christian community has been of political significance. It is still so today, however reluctantly, for the simple reason that as a community it constitutes a group within society.

We owe to modern political theology—and the reasoning is also set out elsewhere in this number of *Concilium*—the realization that the Christian community does not only have a *de facto* political significance but that it also has such significance as a consequence of its understanding of itself. Lenin was speaking within the Hegelian tradition, and was in our opinion quite right, when he wrote: "There is no such thing as an abstract truth; truth is always concrete."[1] The same must be said for the Christian truth. Central values such as love of neighbour, peace, reparation, justification, are values that come from the attitudes and words of Jesus of Nazareth and from the Bible and cannot be understood exclusively in private, spiritual, eschatological or abstract theoretical terms. They have to be made concrete here and now.

The Christian community which knows itself to be bound to Jesus Christ and his message, follows after him and searches sincerely for a Christian orthopraxis which will also acquire a political mandate. But the decisive question is how this political mandate is to be put into effect.

---

[1] *Ausgewählte Werke*, I (Stuttgart, 1957), p. 412; cf. Dorothee Sölle, *Truth is Concrete* (London and New York, 1969).

II. The Christian Community must take sides

Politics cannot be pursued for its own sake. The political involvement of the Christian community has to serve particular objectives. What Jesus said of the law is true also of political commitment—politics was made for man, not man for politics (cf. Mark 2. 27). The meaning and object of political involvement is the humanization of the social reality, the conquest of the various forms of human alienation. When something concerns man, his well-being and his happiness, the Christian community cannot adopt a neutral attitude that might be tantamount to enabling the continuation of injustice. The attitude and words of Jesus show that the Christian community has to side with mankind, for his freedom and human dignity.

But a Christian will share these objectives with all men of goodwill. For the Christian and the Christian community there is a particular form of partisanship, namely a partisanship on behalf of the despised and rejected among men. Jesus' main concern was primarily for those in physical or spiritual need. He wants us to help the poor, the hungry, the dejected, the unloved, the rejected and the despised (cf. Luke 6. 20, 23).

The political commitment of the Christian community must follow Jesus in these aims. It must always be there on behalf of mankind, but above all for the least fortunate. The liturgy of the Christian community consists essentially of this service of man: "for he who does not love his brother whom he has seen, cannot love God whom he has not seen" (1 John 4. 20). But it is also true that reflection on God and involvement in the liturgy is to man's benefit because in the process ideologies are uncovered, power and authority are relativized, and false gods and idols are rendered harmless.

Except in a few particular circumstances, partisanship in this sense does not mean lending support to a particular political party through the medium of the Christian community. The Christian community's campaign on behalf of the oppressed will involve it in debate and argument with all forms of social power that those try to acquire who want to lord it over others instead of helping them to greater freedom and a more complete realization of their humanity. It must be the objective of the Christian community "to change and overthrow all circumstances in which man becomes a humbled, enslaved, rejected and contemptible creature, circumstances that could not be better described than through the words of the Frenchman about to witness the killing of a dog: 'Poor creature! They want to treat you like a human being!'" (Marx).[2]

How does one square partisanship of this type with the Church's mission to act for all people? In siding with the oppressed for the sake of humanity Jesus sides with mankind as a whole. Man is his concern, his well-being, his renewed sense of identity, his liberation and redemption. Thus, when the Christian community steps in on behalf of the underprivileged, its central concern is the salvation of man, the conquest of human failings for the good of a more perfect humanity. With this, something is done for all men, not for the sufferers alone. The Peruvian bishops were therefore right to say in one of their documents: "This means that the Church community in Peru must become involved as individuals and as community on behalf of the oppressed and the rejected. Such involvement will exclude no one from our love. For us to become involved on behalf of the oppressed is an effective way of showing our love for those who perhaps unconsciously, precisely through their role as oppressors, are themselves oppressed."[3]

This fundamental vision of an objective for the political involvement of the Christian community in no way releases it from the need to lay down short and medium term goals that will contribute to the basic aim of the liberation of man. Such short and medium term goals cannot be laid down once and for all but must arise from the common concern of the people. We shall return to this point later. If short term goals are made absolute, the thought system behind it can readily fall into the trap of totalitarianism. Or at the very least the danger exists that such thinking will contribute to an entrenchment of the degree of alienation prevailing at the time.

[2] "Kritik der Hegelschen Rechtsphilosophie", in Karl Marx, *Werke, Schriften, Briefe*, I (Stuttgart, 1962), p. 497.
[3] *Diakonia*, 3 (1972), p. 122.

III. The Binding Force of Political Commitment

The question that we must now consider is, does political action on the part of the community arise from the Christian message and is such action therefore binding on all members of the community? Or is it a question of judging the actual situation and deciding accordingly, and therefore subject to error and binding on no one?

To unravel this point we shall have to examine the criteria on which the political commitment of the Christian community is based. These criteria can be divided into two types. On the one hand there are the standards and impulses provided through the example of Jesus' own behaviour, and on the other hand there are the criteria that come to light through a thorough analysis of the social situation.

Both sets of criteria constitute necessary preconditions for the political involvement of the Christian community. Without a more or less profound understanding of the significance of Jesus and the meaning of his message and the way in which these have been handed on, the community betrays its Lord. Similarly, without the necessary specialized knowledge of the social, economic and political situation, all political action is vain and could actually become counter-productive: instead of helping mankind it could worsen its lot. However well-intentioned political commitment might be it cannot do without an objective and thorough analysis of the overall situation.

At the same time, it would be wrong to argue in purely deductive terms from the message of Jesus to the strategy and tactics of political commitment, as though the one might be supra-naturalistically extrapolated from the other. The message of the New Testament does not provide a finished programme of political action for modern times. Equally, it would be wrong to base political action exclusively on the fruits of an analysis of the current situation. The danger then would be that one would see and act only within the confines of the existing situation. The proper solution is much more in the direction of what Paul Tillich called the method of correlation. In this method, the questions contained within the situation are correlated with the answers contained within the Christian message. The answers are not derived from the questions, nor are there answers that have no connection with the questions. Instead, the method correlates questions and answers, situation and message, human existence and divine self-revelation.[4]

It is clear therefore that the political praxis of the Christian community must be seen in constant connection with Jesus and his message and with the analysis of the present situation. It is as it were a three-cornered situation: political praxis poses questions to the Christian message. This in turn provides certain perspectives for the social analysis. From this consequences arise that affect political praxis, and so on. Between all three elements there must be a permanent dialogue, and all three elements must be mutually critical in their dealings with one another.

Our question concerning the binding force of political commitment for the Christian community can now be answered, at least in outline. In cases where human rights are being crudely trodden underfoot, where particular social structures are in direct confrontation with the Christian message, the Christian community can do nothing other than everything humanly possible to help change the situation through political action. In this situation there is an immediate binding force for all members of the community. Examples of such situations would be cases of open racial discrimination, torturing, starvation, murder, genocide.

In those cases where the political action of the Christian community does not derive quite so unequivocally and directly from Jesus' own teachings but much more from an analysis of the existing situation and of the previous practice of the community, as well as the perspectives and motivations arising from the Christian message, the immediate binding force of political action on each individual member of the community will be reduced or at least it will apply only in so far as the arguments brought forward with respect to a particular form of political action are found convincing. This does not mean that all are free to decide as they please but simply that there must be respect for the conscience of the individual member of the community. The consequences of this for the minorities within the community has still to be discussed.

[4] See Paul Tillich, *Gesammelte Werke*, V (Stuttgart, 1964), p. 142.

IV. Ways in which the Christian Community can be
politically committed

There are many forms of political commitment open to the Christian community. It is not just that the various social situations require differing responses, but also the subject itself will differ from place to place and from time to time. It will be helpful to refer to a few typical situations.

A primary and obvious form consists in the personal political commitment of individual members of the community, undertaken for Christian reasons, in the wide range of political institutions. The political action of the individual Christian undertaken in concert with his fellow citizens, including non-Christians, and with other groups in political parties, trade unions, etc., occurs of course at the individual's own responsibility and risk. But to the extent that he is a member of the community and as such receives from it an understanding of the Christian message that affects his political activity, such action must also be seen in the context of the community as a whole. It is to be hoped that opportunity will be offered within the community for the individual member to discuss the subject of his own political action so that this can be subjected to critical examination on the part of other members of the community to the individual's personal benefit.

The Christian community should also be a place where members of differing political views can come together with a view to thrashing out their differences and for the sake of a better understanding and an ever more effective realization of the gospel message; it will also of course provide opportunity for the common celebration of the Eucharist. The Christian community must show that reconciliation is not just a matter of words but something actively sought within society as a whole.

A second form of political involvement on the part of Christians is provided by certain specific groups who come together either with a particular political action in mind or who are pursuing more long-term political objectives. Such groups might be made up of Christians from a particular community or from various communities, from a particular district or from the country as a whole. As such, these groups are not to be equated with the Christian community. As the members of these groups will be either all or at least for the greater part Christians, will perhaps call themselves such, or at least regard themselves as bound by the Christian message, they will rightly be judged by the public at large on the basis of Christian criteria—this on account of their connection with the Christian community, or with the local or national Church. Such groups will be aware of the responsibility thus placed upon them. Without in fact having an official mandate from the Church, they represent the Church to the public, just as, though to a much lesser extent, the individual Christian does in his own political acts.

In this matter of the political involvement of individual Christians the Church itself and society at large will have to become accustomed to the fact that individual Christians and particular groups will act politically from Christian motivation while at the same time finding themselves on differing sides of the political spectrum. In most instances of political action there is no such thing as a self-evidently Christian programme or solution, which means that it is quite possible that individual Christians or groups of Christians will come up with politically opposed conclusions in answer to a particular concrete political question. This is partly due to differing assessments of the social situation and its needs, and above all of the way in which a political problem ought to be solved. But it is also possible that there will be differing opinions as to the interpretation of the Christian message with regard to the concrete situation in question. It is important in such cases that the Christian, or groups, who disagree about political action in this way do not resort to mutual declarations of heresy or argue that their particular political solution is the one and only Christian solution; rather should they try their best, through debate, to see each other's point of view, but above all they should endeavour to solve the problem at issue in such a way that the greatest number of people gain thereby. What matters particularly is that conflicts of this type between Christians or groups of Christians are not suppressed, that one does not attempt to draw a veil over them, but that one strives to settle them. In this way the conflict can be turned into a dynamic element not only with regard to the particular controversy at issue but also with regard to the life of the Christian community as a

whole, or even that of the Church as a whole.[5] And it is precisely
in the settling of these disputes that one ought to be able to see
whether or not Christians are able to develop such a thing as a
specifically Christian manner of settling their differences.

Political groups motivated by Christian principles are of very
considerable significance in Church and society. For one thing,
when political action results in the successful achievement of
their objectives they will have contributed to an improvement in
the human situation. Secondly, they will thereby have renewed
the presence of the Church within society and given it fresh
credibility. But over and above that, they are in a position to
perform a useful service for the Christian community generally,
in as far as they demonstrate through their action that the gospel
message has political consequences. In other words, they can
assist in the formation of a political consciousness within the
Christian community. Above all they can show unequivocally
that Christianity means stepping in on behalf of the less privileged classes and so help to stir the conscience of the community
and of society as a whole with regard to their responsibility for
deprived people.

Reference should also be made to yet another way in which the
Christian community can become politically involved. In the
face of inhuman acts, when human rights and human dignity
are trodden underfoot, the Christian community has no choice
but to respond, even if this only takes the form of a protest, in
order not through silence to share in the guilt. In such cases, the
community is called upon to do something precisely as community, and no member of the community will be able to absent
himself from the protest if he wishes in the future to profess his
belief in Jesus Christ.

The real problem in this whole matter arises in those cases
where there is no clear connection between the Christian message
and political action. Can a Christian community undertake political action in situations other than those discussed so far? It
seems to me that there are no strong reasons for excluding further political action on the part of the Christian community acting as such. If one is serious in one's contention that belief in

[5] See I. Hermann, "Conflict and Conflict Resolution in the Church",
Concilium, March 1972 (American Edn., vol. 73).

Jesus has political consequences, and if one bears in mind the fact that even political neutrality—if there is such a thing—can itself be a political act, and when it is recalled that every truth, and particularly a Christian truth, must make sense in real terms if it is to retain the quality of truth, then in particular circumstances one would concede the possibility of there being such a thing as legitimate concrete political involvement on the part of the Christian community. It must be said though that the most important condition for such political action would be the democratization of the community.

V. Democratization as a Precondition

In discussing the question of the democratization of the Christian community, it is not intended that one should simply and uncritically apply to the Church any model of the democratic structure taken at random from the civil sphere. Rather is the expression used to indicate a process in the course of which ever more definite principles, attitudes, forms of behaviour, structures, and forms of law become established, all of which will serve to overcome human alienation, above all to exchange the direct rule of one man by another for the rational exercise of power, and in this way assist mankind towards freedom and happiness.[6]

In arguing here that a democratization of the community is a precondition for political commitment on the part of that community one has already caught hold of an important aspect of the democratization process. The community can only engage in concrete political action precisely as a community when such political action has been preceded by an intensive growth of political consciousness, a process in which opinions have been formed, and a democratic decision-making procedure established. This is the decisive point at which the traditional form of Christian integralism is to be distinguished from the type of political involvement under discussion. In the past, it was an ecclesiastical official, or a committee of such officials, who decided what political objectives Catholics should support, what political parties they should back, and what individuals they should vote

[6] See *Concilium*, March 1971 (American Edn., vol. 63), on the theme of the democratization of the Church.

for. But what we are talking about now is how a Christian community together with its ordained leader copes with a matter of public concern, analyses and assesses a particular situation, gathers the necessary information, discusses the political problems, and then together reaches a decision. In concrete terms, that means that the precondition for a programme of political action on the part of the community is a system of community meetings at which political problems can be aired, also the existence of work study groups to collect and analyse information, and the existence of democratically elected representative committees able to do the groundwork and authorized to make some decisions themselves, and a community leadership that does not act authoritatively but instead prepares the way towards collective decisions.

The fact that in many of our communities this sort of democratization process simply has not yet got off the ground should not cause us to underrate its importance. Only to the extent that the community is democratized in this way will it experience success in its political undertakings. For a community that is led in an authoritarian way does not readily achieve political consciousness, though it soon enough accepts a political ideology anxious to protect the *status quo* at all costs. But then it must be said that the only type of community that is really entitled to act as such in a political context is one that has reached a political decision democratically—however heated the preceding debate may have been.

We now have to face the question posed by the existence within a community of a minority whose opinion on a particular issue cannot be represented in the conclusion finally reached. This problem cannot be solved in general terms but one would accept as a principle the statement that the more important the decision to be reached the larger must be the majority. To put that in more concrete terms—the question as to whether a community should instal a new carillon or whether it should not use the money instead for the building of houses for immigrant workers could well be settled by a simple majority and the disappointed minority will have to live with the decision according to the custom of democratic behaviour. But whether or not a community acts as such in solidarity with a group of striking employees, offering them financial and moral support, or what party a community should side with when it comes to a decisive political vote, simply cannot be decided on the basis of 51 against and 49 in favour. Should a community decide to take up a position on major political issues, then one would expect to see a significant majority, if not actual unanimity, or something approaching it very closely. Should this not at first prove possible then those involved would have to revert to internal discussion in the hope of achieving unity after all; or, if the situation seems to require it, the parties could agree to withdraw from political involvement on this point altogether.

A disappointed minority will find it that much easier to remain members of the community if it is as clear to the community as to the public that a particular political and community decision, though it emerged from general and Christian motivation, is not *the* Christian solution, or is not necessarily so. The community may have adopted a particular course of action but it will not argue that all other Christians must do likewise. On the other hand, there is always the possibility that a member of the community or a group of such members who find themselves more or less frequently frustrated can leave and instead join some other community.

VI. The Specific Character of Christian Political Commitment

The heading of this section is not intended to suggest that there are particular insights or fundamental modes of behaviour peculiar to Christians. On the contrary, the intention is to point to a few tendencies typifying Christian political action and arising from the Christian message. If Christians and non-Christians are able to agree in these matters, then so much the better.

Political commitment on the part of Christians is based on confidence in mankind. This trust can be disappointed though it could not justify in the Christian a display of fundamentally suspicious attitudes. Foresight and wisdom are not thereby excluded, but the Christian will assume that the man he is dealing with is equally capable of perceiving what is right, and that he has an open mind and that he is capable of changing it. This at least was the attitude of Jesus of Nazareth towards his fellow men.

The Christian will give his fellow man time to think. He will not apply any pressure, or attempt to manipulate him through the use of superior power or tactics. He asks the other to act in accordance with the gospel message, just as he is trying to do. Political involvement on the part of the Christian contains within it an invitation to the other.

The Christian who is serious about following Christ through his political concern will always strive to act in concert with the other, however warped his political awareness. The Christian will always respect his fellow man. In this regard, the political commitment of the Christian is most obviously distinguished from that of the Marxist, or at least from that of certain Marxist movements. If God himself so respects man's freedom that he allows him even the freedom to commit sin, man will also have to respect the freedom of the other, even when he is quite convinced that he is abusing his freedom.

The Christian will show through his political involvement that he appreciates his duty to contribute all his powers for the benefit of a more human world. However, he will approach things calmly because he knows that the completion of all things is in the safe hands of a far greater reality than he is. For this reason the Christian will rejoice in even partial successes.

Political involvement on the part of the Christian must show that it is possible to side with the underprivileged without at the same time demonstrating group egoism. The goal cannot be the replacement of one establishment by another, instead of the dictatorship of established powers the dictatorship of the proletariat. The concern must be to assist the individual person less well off than his fellows, and underprivileged groups, to a position of equal partnership in society, and to eliminate altogether situations in which one man can lord it over another.

In all this, the absence of violence must be a fundamental characteristic. This is clear from the words and actions of Jesus himself. This does not mean that one must do nothing, or that one has an alibi for the resigned acceptance of oppression. But a decisive action, the non-violent provocation, is certainly much more in accordance with Jesus' own attitudes than the unconsidered use of force. This does not mean that there are not borderline cases in which even the Christian is forced into a position of adopting the use of revolutionary violence. Pope Paul VI did not exclude such a likelihood. He clearly thought the same when, in *Populorum progressio*, 21, he wrote: "Every revolutionary uprising—except in the case of the clear and longstanding abuse of power which damages the basic rights of the individual and the general good of the country—gives rise to fresh injustice." And in a declaration on behalf of the Third World by fifteen Catholic bishops we read: "Not all revolutions are necessarily good. . . . But history shows that certain revolutions were necessary so that those concerned could free themselves from anti-religious elements, and that these revolutions have borne good fruit."[7] But when Christians use violence in order to push through their objectives, this must only occur as a last resort. Christians must be fully aware of the enormous responsibility such a course places upon them, for revolutionary actions can readily introduce fresh human misery. The use of violence must be considered admissible only in the most extreme borderline situations.

The Christian should always subject his own political actions to careful scrutiny. He must always ensure that his aims are right ones, that his methods suit the situation and are in keeping with the requirements of Christian observance, and he must test them for effectiveness. He will also be open to criticism from others. He will never strive in an authoritarian way for a short-term objective, or insist on the use of methods he happens to have chosen. He will keep an open mind at all times and will remain flexible to the extent that he is able to withdraw from a particular course of action when it is shown to be wrong or ineffective. In this way Christian political action will have the character of an experiment, without however becoming merely arbitrary. In this sense, the Christian will also be prepared to undertake calculated risks. This will ensure that he does not so concentrate on an examination of theory as to forget the nature of action.

Throughout his political activities the Christian must be willing to merge his interest with those of others, to form coalitions. He will regard co-operation with other Christians, or with groups of Christians, or with Christian communities of a different confession, as a matter of course. He will also be prepared to

[7] Quoted from T. Rendtorff and H. E. Tödt, *Theologie der Revolution* (Frankfurt, 1968), p. 158.

co-operate with non-Christians where there is agreement on objective and method. He will not undertake projects unaided just for the sake of making a show if he is aware that co-operation with others would be much more effective.

Decisive at all times will be whether or not the political commitment of the Christian community in this or that form is in accord with the needs of the situation and the requirements of those on whose behalf the action is planned, as also whether or not the action is undertaken in the spirit of Jesus Christ. These tests must be applied on each individual occasion, not just once and for all.

VII. The Political Education of the Community

Before a Christian community can become politically involved, it usually has to undergo a lengthy process of political education. Learning means undergoing change through experience and understanding. Thus it is important that the Christian community should fully understand that the realization of the Christian faith does not take place in a world of its own existing alongside the day-to-day life of man. This must be made clear right from the start in all forms of catechetics, not excluding the use of the mass media. It is even more important that the community should reflect upon its own experiences in the light of the gospel message. This process can begin among the community members: the needs of the elderly, the sick, immigrants, released prisoners, unmarried mothers, drug addicts, and so on. Every Christian community must be prepared to offer help to such people, whether in their own community or outside it. In these contacts it will be discovered that although direct assistance is indispensable, and perhaps in the future will become even more so, in many cases long-term help is only effective when specific structures are altered, when the need in question is met institutionally. But this would only be possible through political action. Of course it is important and necessary to give the children of immigrant workers special instruction in the host language so that they can hold their own in school, but at the same time it is important to institute those structural changes that will enable such immigrant workers as wish it to become more fully integrated into the life around them.

Political education through practical experience of this type, gathered through looking to the needs of one's fellow men, is considerably more effective than mere theoretical debate. Of course there will also be a theoretical discussion but this will be undertaken in connection with the problems being faced in practice.

Important to this learning process within the community is the tolerance of frustration. The man whose approach to a particular problem is utopian, or who sets himself illusory goals, will very soon give up. Putting up with frustration does not mean adaptation and acceptance but involves the understanding that a certain degree of frustration is part of the human condition and that provided it is mastered it can become the driving force towards renewed effort. It means that though one is prepared for failure one is not deterred by it.

Political action among the needy, as described above, provides the possibility from time to time at least of being able to experience a few successes—particularly if the initial goals are not set too high. Both—the experience of success and the tolerance of frustration—are important factors in the political learning process.

VIII. CONCLUSION

The Church will only achieve a fresh credibility when it unequivocally abandons an ideological justification for social injustices and, in the imitation of Christ, takes action on behalf of mankind generally, siding clearly and at all times with the underprivileged. It is here that the political commitment of the Christian community matters. Action in this regard will win them neither power nor influence but instead contempt, threats and persecution from the ruling class. But they will be in good company, for such was the position of Jesus himself.[8]

That such political involvement on the part of the Church is necessary is shown by the statement put out by the Peruvian hierarchy in its paper "Towards a Just World": "The Peruvian

[8] See Adolf Holl, *Jesus in Bad Company* (London and New York, 1972).

Church exists in a country that stands at an historic turning-point at which the people are decided to build up a more just society.... In response to this situation there are those in the Christian community who support the cause of the oppressed, identifying themselves with their problems, their struggles and their expectations. For many Christians, this involvement is made easier by a theology that regards the condition of the oppressed peoples as sinful and as a contempt of God's plan, and that sees the support of their freedom movement as a response to the Lord's call to fashion history through active participation. The Church is discovering that by virtue of its presence it is inescapably involved in politics and that it cannot spread the Gospel in a situation of widespread oppression without first of all awakening the conscience of the people by presenting the message of Jesus Christ, who sets men free."[9]

Translated by Mark Hollebone

[9] *Diakonia*, 3 (1972), pp. 120, 122.

Hugo Assmann

Political Commitment in the Context of the Class Struggle

VARIOUS Christian groups in Latin America are now stressing the notion of "class struggle" in their political thought. The purpose of this short article is to analyse briefly some characteristic aspects and some of the determining causes of their use of this concept. Our central reference point can be those groups of Christians who formed the majority of the four hundred delegates of the First Latin American Conference on "Christians for Socialism", and who agree with the "Final Statement" of this conference.[1] From this central point we may broaden our enquiry to cover the wide-spread but ambiguous use of the term "liberation", a political answer to the socio-analytical term "dependence" in economic development. These groups are very conscious of the fact that they are new and few in members in the Church. They are therefore not inclined at the moment to euphoria. Their situation encourages, on the contrary, a sharp self-criticism and much free discussion within the groups, that is to say, between those who agree with their aims.

It would be revealing to analyse the growing class-consciousness and corresponding political language of any one particular group. But this would require a much more detailed analysis of local politics,[2] which is beyond the scope of this article. This

[1] Santiago de Chile, 23–30 April 1972. See the material in *Cristianos por el socialismo* (Santiago, 1972; Buenos Aires, 1972; Milan, 1972). See also the list of incomplete editions especially *Documento Final*, in the prologue of the book; later repercussions in *Cristianismo y Sociedad* (1972).

[2] Cf. J. Bengoa, *Lucha de clases y consciencia de clases* (Santiago, 1972);

means, however, that our approach must be general and that we cannot be as particular as we should like.

I. CHARACTERISTICS OF THE USAGE OF THE TERM "CLASS STRUGGLE"

The first point we should mention is that this term forms part of the whole network of social and theological ideas of these left-wing Christians. This means that it is impossible to isolate the term "class struggle" without distorting it. No language arising from a particular practice or way of life, and whose purpose is to be a means for the discussion of that practice, can suffer any one of its terms to be analysed out of context in an abstract meta-physical way. To do this would be to do violence to it.

Such a language cannot be properly understood from "outside" its own presuppositions. This is not an arbitrary "red light" but the very nature of such a "situated" language. Otherwise, mistakes are bound to be made. For example, it is unlikely that an international congress of "progressive" theologians, in which there is no agreement on the meaning of the term "under-development", and its fundamental redefinition as "depen-dence", would be in a position to discuss the meaning of the term "liberation" as used in many of the theological writings of Latin America,[3] or indeed the exact sense of "class struggle" in the "Final Statement" of the Santiago Conference.

The term "class struggle" is thus a technical term within a schema, and its technical or scientific propriety depends entirely on the weakness or strength of this schema as a whole. One of the most common mistakes is to say that Marx created an absolutely new principle for the explanation of the world, an absolute theory of "class struggle". This term is an expressly historical category and in Marx's writings, for example his famous letter to Weyde-meyer in March 1852, it is explicitly connected with particular stages of the development of production.

The horror felt by many Christians for "class struggle" often

---

E. Munoz, *La legitimación del sistema de clases* (Santiago, 1972). Both studies analyse particular groups.

[3] Cf. G. Gutierrez, *Teología de la liberación*. Perspectivas (Lima, 1972; Salamanca, 1972); H. Assmann, *Opresión-Liberación. Desafío a los cristianos* (Montevideo, 1971); bibliography in *Iglesia y cambio social en América Latina* (Salamanca, 1972).

arises from a misunderstanding of the term. They wrongly suppose that this term implies a state of conflict always and everywhere to be part of "human nature" or that it is even some sort of mystical alternative to divine providence; this is because they do not understand the particular and historical nature of the "class struggle" and of "class" itself in Marxist thought.

In the Latin American texts, particularly the "Final Statement" referred to above, the term "class struggle" is clearly set within a fairly detailed analysis of the dependent state of our countries. A mainly descriptive analysis of exploitation, as in the writings of Medellín (1968), has now been superseded as inadequate, together with the general denunciations which usually followed these descriptions. The progress of the social sciences in America has gradually laid bare the structural causes of our situation as subject peoples, and has led to an economic and political reassessment of our past and present. These socio-analytical findings, the key to which are the notions of "dependence" and "unequal development", are far from being a closed system of a certain popular Marxist kind. The analysis is far more demanding and qualified than this, although of course its essential categories are Marxist. Among us today there is no doubt that Marxism is in a vigorous process of critical deepening and development.

All this must be borne in mind before reading the texts of groups of revolutionary Christians. A familiarity with some popular Marxist ideas will not be sufficient to understand them. We must suppose that several of these texts are known to our readers and so do not give examples. We shall see later how a simplistic reductionism (to popular Marxism) is the most common mode of criticism used by the conservative Church which opposes these groups.

A second characteristic of the use of the term "class struggle" in these texts is its reference to the present situation. There is frequent mention of the "sharpening of the class struggle" and a description of the structural causes why the international and national capitalist system must strengthen its means of self-defence and attack. There is thus an awareness of the particular determinants of the present situation. Although the class struggle on a world scale is not discussed in detail, it is constantly present in these texts.

Another basic characteristic is that class confrontation is firmly removed from the false context of "morality" or feelings and intentions, which leads to its absurd identification with hatred. This is why the infra-structural causes are principally stressed, but not, as we shall see, exclusively. But they also hold that "the class struggle cannot be reduced to a purely economic and social struggle; it is also ideological".[4] "Structures" are therefore not made out to be abstract combatants, although the objective structural causes are pointed out. The dominant rather than the dominated are named as the *cause* of the struggle, that is to say they are chiefly "responsible" for the violence involved. The frequent "Christian" transposition of this responsibility from the oppressors to the oppressed is simply absurd. Such presuppositions can tell us much about what side someone who uses this schema is on. Traditional "Christian" criticism of this precise point in Marxist revolutionary theory habitually reverses the responsibility for the struggle.

This happens particularly when "class struggle" is considered as a strategy. It is in discussion of strategy that these traditional "Christians" habitually reverse the responsibility. It is therefore a radical restatement for Latin American Christians in the above-mentioned texts to stress constantly that the "guilty" in the class conflict are the dominant, and fundamentally, the class structure of society itself. The oppressed have no option but to devise a strategy to change the real and objective conflicts which are the rules of the domination game. To fail to do this would be to accept domination as an unchangeable fact, a natural destiny, and not as an historical fact with historical causes.

In this context it is easier to understand the round assertions in some of these texts; they are not just slogans. "The historical process of class society and imperialist domination results in a necessary class confrontation." "The present situation of all the people on this continent, and in the end of all Christians, consciously or unconsciously, is determined by the historical dynamism of the class struggle in the liberation process." "The recognition of the class struggle as a fundamental fact enables us

[4] *Documento Final, op. cit.*, 54; for this and the following paragraphs see also *Cristianismo y Sociedad, op. cit.*, and *Pasos. Un documento de reflexión por semana*, ISAL (Santiago, all 1972 issues).

to arrive at a full interpretation of the structures of Latin America. Revolutionary practice shows us that any objective and scientific interpretation must use class analysis as its principle."[5]

It is quite logical that it should be revolutionary Christians who are particularly interested in the ideological aspects of the "class struggle", while not forgetting the infra-structural socio-economic facts. Their ideological interest can probably be explained by their daily experience of the terrible blindness in heart and conscience of so many Christians to the fact of the class struggle. We refer to the resistance by such "Christians" to giving their energies to revolutionary change.

This is why it is so important to attack this ideological disagreement in an open manner. The "sharpening of the class struggle" means a new stage of the ideological political struggle and admits of no neutrality or withdrawal from politics. But because the "class struggle is also an ideological struggle" we must see that "the reason for the blindness of most people to the class struggle is the class struggle itself", and that "one of the most important aims of the ideological struggle is to name and remove the disguise from so-called Christian justifications (of the dominant class)". On the one hand, it is stated that "an inadequate understanding of the class struggle has led many Christians to be insufficiently involved politically", which is why they support Christian democrat type politics. On the other hand, it is also stressed in the "Final Statement" that it is not merely a work of improving man's understanding, because "it is *praxis* (action) with the proletariat that removes the blindness of heart and mind and involves Christians in the class struggle. This blindness, with its history, is itself an important factor in the cultural revolution."[6]

One last aspect, which should be obvious, but is not always so for Christians caught between systems, is that to engage in the class struggle strategically does not mean that this struggle is regarded as the essence of man and human history. On the contrary, to refuse to recognize the existing conflicts in class society means accepting them as a state of "nature". To accept the "class

[5] *Ibid.*, 24, 27, 48.
[6] *Ibid.*, 29, 62, 56, 53, 44; cf. also *Pasos*, 16 (1972), report on the one-day conference, "Gospel and class struggle".

struggle" means putting it in its proper place, in history, that is to say, accepting it as one of the facts which are unfortunately true, but which can and should be changed. In other words, accepting the "class struggle" is the first step on the way to resolving it. It is therefore quite false to object, on "Christian" grounds, that those who engage in the "class struggle" in order to overthrow the class society from which it arises, makes this struggle an absolute. "Faith makes it all the more necessary that the class struggle should be fought and won to free all mankind, in particular those who are most bitterly oppressed."[7]

Because we must be brief, we cannot go into detail here of the theological strength of these groups in their description of the state of being caught between the systems in which the central doctrines of Christianity now lie. The "Final Statement" we have quoted begins with the explicit assertion that its authors are Christians. Certain official quarters of the churches expressed their surprise that "people like that" should still be seriously concerned with their Christian faith. . . .

II. Determining Causes of this View of the "Class Struggle"

We give here some of the reasons why such groups are so aware of the "class struggle". We shall speak in general terms and not give biographical details. The reader will realize that everything we say has to be greatly expanded.

The first fact is the living experience of these groups politically committed to conflicts in their various countries. This is why their writings constantly stress in a more theoretical way the "epistemological density of praxis". Behind each reflection there are numerous painful experiences.

But there are also evolutionary stages in their awareness. Let me enumerate some of the factors that have played a part in this. The post-conciliar and post-Medellín euphoria has rapidly evaporated. The groups have come to terms with the central and apolitical position of Vatican II and have seen how it is adapted to the present stage of capitalism. They have become disappointed with "progressive" North Atlantic theologians and their support of the system. They have witnessed the "withdrawal from history"

[7] *Ibid.*, 65.

of these theologies, even the most politically committed. Social action in the churches has become restricted to mere "modernizing". That heterogeneous body of work called the "social doctrine of the Church" has now reached a crisis of impotence in its general denunciations and particularly in its blessing of "interclassism" and "third positions". These groups are conscious of the theologically and politically reactionary nature of some postconciliar reformism and of the growing distance of "European theology" from anything satisfactory for Latin America. As a final example, we may mention the poor record of Christian democracy in the Latin American countries. This is a bare list, without any order, of general causes. I have not indicated their effects on individuals.

But what has all this to do with the growing awareness of the "class struggle"? In our view, a great deal. Through these and other similar events, people have come to see how blind the Churches and their theologians have been to the revolutionary challenge. It is symptomatic of their attitude that they suggest, as objects of charity, problems which do not bring the question of class conflict in society plainly to the fore. Some of the problems chosen, for example, are peace, hunger, underdevelopment,[8] the arms race, migration and torture. Anything you like, including "liberating education",[9] so long as the "class struggle" is not mentioned. There are well-known progressive ways of representing the capitalist theology and it is well known that the Churches and theology today are important "proving grounds" for the system to try to recapture ideologically people's hopes for change. Even if we dismiss the simple line that the Church is merely an "instrument of imperialism", and accept its peculiar religious function, there is still plenty of room to question what the churches "do" in the politics of being caught between the systems.

The basic fact is that the highest officialdom of the churches

[8] For an idea of the reactionary ideology of most of the organizations for aid in their use of the concept "underdevelopment", cf. *Dossier comparatif des options relatives au développement* (Centre Protestant d'Etudes et Documentations, Nov. 1970); and material on the profound crisis in *Justitia et Pax* and SODEPAX.

[9] Cf. P. Freire, "El papel educativo de las Iglesias en América Latina", in *Contacto* (Mexico, Sept. 1972).

continues to claim that they are above social conflict.[10] The fundamentally tragic and desperate character[11] of many attempts at a theology of hope which do not include fighting for that hope which is essential for it to survive, clearly shows the insufficiency of such a vague political theology. To lay bare the ideological function of a claim by the churches and theology to be apolitical is merely the first stage of the problem, which is much more complicated than this; it is the structuring of faith by the political at the level of historical options. In the first stage of the problem, many things have become evidence for the Christian groups we mentioned. For example, the fact that the current versions of Christian universalism—universal love, reconciliation, love of enemies, etc.—have become caught and tamed by liberal bourgeois ideology, so that they frequently hide the close connection between social conflicts and the internal conflicts of the Church.[12] Thus it has become impossible for the Church to understand and give its true message because it will not consciously accept the fact of its dependence on and duty to become involved in social conflicts; the Christian can no longer live a "parallel life".

There is a need for a far deeper study of the exact correlation between the mechanisms of domination of class society and the exact way in which these mechanisms impinge on the historical expression of faith by the Church. In other words, is there always and inevitably a link between theory and practice, and indeed total political strategy, in the historical expression of the faith which is visibly embodied in the Church? The question does not appear to have arisen yet in this form for the Christian groups mentioned above. However, they implicitly reply to this question by expressly choosing the united theory and practice, socio-analytical and theological, forming precisely a strategical total, of opposing intra-systemic reformism, that is to say of embracing socialism.

[10] This aspect is fully analysed in J. Guichard, *Eglise, lutte de classes et stratégies politiques* (Paris, 1972); and J. Girardi, *Christianisme, libération humaine et lutte des classes* (Parsi, 1972).

[11] See the chapter entitled "Théologie et tragédie", in A. Gouhier, *Pour une métaphysique du pardon* (Paris, 1969), pp. 361–400.

[12] Cf. *Documento Final*, esp. part II; H. Assmann, "El cristianismo, su plusvalia ideologica y el costo social de la revolucion socialista", in *Cuadernos de la Realidad Nacional* (Santiago, April 1972), pp. 154–79.

Growing awareness of this chosen way raises sooner or later the really fundamental question—is the historically effective role of Christianity and the structuring of faith by the political necessarily connected with the Word, heard here and now historically, and the possibility of hearing and doing this Word, not just in vague "signs of the times" but in a much closer way? Is it connected by reading this Word in the light of a particular ethically determined social analysis, a particular total ethical-political strategy, and so in an essentially historically determined way? We believe that this kind of fundamental question will have to be asked more and more often by Christians. In this, theology, in its usual sense of "expert profession", will surely be radically impotent, because the need will arise for a new theological praxis defined from within revolutionary praxis, the subject of which cannot be primarily the individual theologian but must be the Christian group involved in revolution.

However, there are also more immediate tasks which cannot be postponed. Almost the whole of "official Christianity" is still so blind to the problem of the "class struggle" that we must begin humbly and patiently, in an introductory way, to explain to them.... At the moment it is still politically important to repeat with great patience things which for many are quite obvious.

Let me conclude by giving one particular example. The core of the resistance is theoretically weak and uses a highly emotive reductionist schema. Anxious Pope Paul, certain frightened Latin American bishops, the theoretical organs of Christian democracy, the ultra right press, and also clearly P. R. Vekemans, that clever manager, all rely on exactly the same simplistic formula: the "theology of liberation" is reduced, by constant confused statements, simply and plainly to a "theology of violence" and "violence" of course is synonymous with "hatred". Christianity is a religion of "love", so let no one speak to us about "conflicts", let alone "class struggle".[13]

Translated by Dinah Livingstone

[13] Many comparative texts in H. Assmann, "La ideología burguesa sus piezas de recambio religiosas", *Casa de las Américas* (Havana, 1972).

Michael Traber

The Church's Political Commitment in the Racial Conflict

I. The Racial Conflict

"RACE", "racism", "racial conflict", and so on, are rather vague concepts with many shades of meaning, and our first task is to explain them.

Biology divides living creatures into species, and this term is defined essentially as a group capable of reproducing itself. In this sense biology regards all human beings living today as clearly belonging to the species *homo sapiens*. The species is subdivided into races or varieties, that is, groups of individuals distinguishable from other groups or races in the same species by shared, genetically determined physical characteristics. In the nineteenth century the biological concept of race was extended to social and cultural characteristics. The influence of Charles Darwin helped to popularize this theory, according to which not only the physical features characteristic of race, but also cultural, social and psychological characteristics were determined by heredity.

In sociology, racism is the term used for relations between different ethnic groups. An ethnic group is a number of human beings who feel themselves to be connected, are regarded by others as being connected, and possess certain physical characteristics which make this connection visible. These characteristics may be biological, such as skin colour or facial characteristics, or social, such as language, religion, clothes or gestures. If a group has no external characteristics, a situation may occur in which these are artificially created, as, for example, the yellow Star of David in Nazi Germany. The function of external characteristics is not just to make the group visible, but also to stimulate prejudices. Prejudices are mistaken judgments based on various stereotyped ideas or images which determine the attitude of their holders towards the group, which then becomes an "out-group". Prejudices can lead to discrimination, that is, a treatment which places the group at a disadvantage. The most acute form of racial discrimination is segregation. In practice racial discrimination means that equality of opportunity is accepted only within one's own group, and, in relations between groups, is abolished for the benefit of the dominant group. Discrimination is expressed not only in social customs, but also to a certain extent in laws governing the economy, education and civil rights. In the last two or three decades it has come to be accepted that political emancipation is the key to racial equality, in other words, that equality of opportunity must first be secured in political rights before it can be implemented in other fields.

The distinguishing feature of the problem of race is that group polarization is always and everywhere visible in clear physical characteristics. The physical characteristics are ineradicable even when the particular individual or group has accepted the values and norms of another group. In the case of racism skin colour becomes a symbol of superiority and inferiority. Skin colour serves as an all-embracing criterion by means of which the whole human population can be categorized and polarized; this is what gives the race problem its peculiar intensity.

In recent times the term "political racism" has been introduced. Two uses of the term can be distinguished: "on the one hand the racism which received its most terrible expression in Nazi Germany", and on the other hand "racism in the form of a political theory closely connected with socialist ideals and tactics".[1] Only the second form of political racism, which is also called white macroethnocentrism,[2] will be briefly examined here. Whereas in the case of racism as an ethnic social category there is always a possibility "that only individuals or individual groups in a population might be implicated in racial attitudes, the thesis

[1] H. Treinen, "Rasse in makrosoziologischer Sicht", in K.-M. Beckmann (ed.), *Rasse, Kirche und Humanum* (Gütersloh, 1969), p. 117.
[2] R. Preiswerk, *Entwicklungshilfe als Kulturbegegnung* (Nuremberg and Fribourg, 1972), pp. 23 ff.

of structural and institutionalized racism maintains that the whole world and all its social institutions is trapped in this theoretical and practical schema. This forms the basic structure of political and economic structures, and originates in the confrontation between black and white."[3] This conception of race is a combination of two elements, the exploitation (or discrimination against) the countries whose development is blocked (the "Third World"), most of which can be placed in a single racial category, by the "white North", and secondly, the application and partial extension of the theories of classes and imperialism developed by Lenin and Rosa Luxemburg, according to which white supremacy is an essential element in the capitalist system of the industrialized countries. This political concept has since also been applied to the socialist and communist states of the East in the same way as previously to the West. The equality demanded by the "coloured world" in this context cannot be understood simply in the (capitalist) sense of the equality of opportunity, but only in the (socialist) sense of restitution, redistribution of wealth and power.

Racism as an expression of political tactics is based on the principle of human rights proclaimed by the United Nations, which are to be understood not only as individual rights but also as rights of groups.[4] But this basic value, shared by black and white, does not mean the abolition of polarization by skin colour, but rather gives it even greater force. This fundamental assessment of human worth makes political actions which form a counterpart to ideas of racial superiority morally defensible. By means of this theory the victims of discrimination can exercise political pressure without the whites being able to offer an acceptable justification for resistance. The whites, who acknowledge the same values, can also act for the benefit of the "oppressed". The new racism thus has a number of implications. On the one hand, a system of values is generally accepted which is based on equality, self-determination, human rights and a sharing of the

[3] K. P. Blaser, *Wenn Gott schwarz wäre. . . . Das Problem des Rassismus in Theologie und christlicher Praxis* (Zürich and Fribourg, 1972), pp. 32–3.
[4] See Chapters XI–XIII of the United Nations Charter and Resolution 1514 (14 Dec. 1960) on Decolonialization.

earth's resources, while, on the other hand, racial discrimination continues to be tolerated. This discrepancy between theory and practice is the characteristic feature of the political problem of race or white racism.

According to the "Church and Society Committee" of the Fourth General Assembly of the World Council of Churches at Uppsala: "We believe, however, that white racism has special historical significance because its roots lie in powerful, highly developed countries, the stability of which is crucial to any hope for international peace and development. The racial crisis in these countries is to be taken as seriously as the threat of nuclear war. The revolt against racism is one of the most inflammatory elements of the social revolution now sweeping the earth; it is fought at the level of mankind's deepest and most vulnerable emotions—the universal passion for human dignity. The threatened internal chaos of those countries in which racial conflict is most intense has immediate world-wide impact, for racism under attack tends to generate and to spread counter-racism."[5]

The front line of the racial conflict has moved in recent years from the U.S.A. to southern Africa. The criticisms of the white racial oligarchies of South Africa—Namibia, Rhodesia and the Portuguese territories of Angola, Mozambique and Guinea-Bissao—today involve much more than pressure for reforms in favour of the black majority. The power relations in these countries are for the non-white peoples a physical proof of the structural racism which dominates the world. The South African model, with its population figures and corresponding income relations, is a microcosm of the present world situation with its contrast between rich and poor. It reflects the whole world problem of racism. It is a test case against which the attitude of the "white North" to the whole Third World is judged. The sale of arms to South Africa, financial support for the Cabora-Bassa hydro-electric project in Mozambique, failure to observe economic sanctions against Rhodesia, the military links between N.A.T.O. and Portugal, trade relations with South Africa, these are the criteria by which both Western and Eastern nations are judged. It is also

[5] *Report from Uppsala. Official Report on the Fourth General Assembly of the World Council of Churches* (London, 1968), pp. 241-2.

by its involvement with or opposition to racism in southern Africa that the credibility of Christianity is measured.

II. THE CHURCH'S COMMITMENT

What is the position of the Church and Christian tradition with regard to racism and the struggle for racial justice? The basic principles of Christian teaching makes it completely opposed to racism in any form. Congar refers in particular to the catholicity and universality of the Church, and calls racism a pseudo-religion which destroys the heart of Christianity, love of neighbour, but he ends his discussion of racial differences with the remark, "in practice the realization of the highest human values seems to be linked to the white race".[6] The Second Vatican Council is even clearer: "The Church rejects any form of discrimination against a man or any act of violence against him on account of his race, colour, class or religion" (Declaration on Non-Christian Religions, *Nostra Aetate*, 5; see also the Constitution on the Church in the Modern World, *Gaudium et Spes*, 29). It can nevertheless be said that "Catholic theology as a whole and Catholic moral theology in particular have made little contribution to the discussion of the racial question".[7] The same holds for Protestant theology, although here the influence of the Geneva headquarters of the World Council of Churches on the examination of the racial problem marks a clear advance over the position of Catholic theology.[8]

Important as it is to subject the problem of race to close theological examination, the Church cannot leave it at that. As a Protestant conference remarked, "There are more than enough statements, resolutions and publications on racism—they all condemn it and call for programmes to eradicate this plague of modern humanity. What is now urgently needed are actions, vigorous and far-reaching actions."[9] The World Council of Churches has recognized this clearly and has set up a "Pro-

---

[6] Y. Congar, *L'Eglise catholique devant la question raciale* (Paris, 1953).
[7] A. Plangger, "Rassenfrage und Missionierung in Rhodesien (1890–1930)", in J. Baumgartner (ed.), *Vermittlung zwischenkirchlicher Gemeinschaft* (Schöneck-Beckenried, 1971), p. 166.
[8] Cf. Blaser, *op. cit.*, pp. 42–50.
[9] J. Vincent, *The Race Race* (London, 1970).

gramme to Fight Racism and Apartheid" with considerable resources of both money and manpower. This programme has
deeply disturbed white Protestant Christianity—and has substan-
tially increased the credibility of the Church in the eyes of the
underprivileged coloureds. This programme recognizes the
reality of political racism. The financial allocations are intended
as a symbolic restitution to the racial outcasts and redistribution
of power. Above all, the race programme has shown that actions
are a much more effective witness on the part of the Church than
purely verbal testimonies.

At a local level, active political commitment on the race question also exists within the Catholic Church. The efforts of the
religious orders to help the American Indians in the sixteenth and
seventeenth centuries, Cardinal Lavigerie's fight for the abolition
of slavery, and the involvement of American Christians in the
race problem in this century cannot be discussed here, as this
article is limited to the political actions of the Church in southern
Africa.

The first colonizers of the African continent, the Portuguese,
are also its last; in Mozambique, Angola and Guinea-Bissao they
maintain a system of structural racism controlled from Lisbon.
Through the Concordat between the Vatican and Portugal (1940)
and the supplementary missionary agreement (1941), the highest
ranks of the Church's leadership are involved in Portuguese
racism, and individual bishops and priests even officially defend
and support the Portuguese system of domination. What a burden
this position is for the Church is shown by the action of the
White Fathers in voluntarily withdrawing from Mozambique in
protest against the collaboration between Church and State in
that country.[10] Individual bishops and priests in the Portuguese
African territories have shown a high degree of political commitment, notably the late Bishop of Beira (Mozambique), Sebas-
tiao de Rezende, who died in 1964, the Vicar General of the
diocese of Luanda (Angola), J. Pinto de Andrade, who is at
present in prison in Portugal, and three priests from Beira, who
were expelled from Mozambique in 1972. The force of these

[10] See *Portugal in Afrika. Analyse eine Befreiungskampfes* (Nuremberg
and Fribourg, 1971), pp. 124 ff. French original, *Dossier sur les colonies
portugaises* (Brussels, 1971).

men's witness is nevertheless considerably reduced by the ambi-valent position—or even counter-testimony—of the episcopate and clergy in Portugal itself. Political observers are unanimous in the view that the Roman Catholic hierarchy occupies a key position in the fight for racial justice in Portuguese Africa. A first step would be the annulment of the Concordat between the Vatican and Portugal and new appointments to most episcopal sees in Mozambique, Angola and Guinea-Bissao.

The episcopate and many priests in South Africa have taken a clearer position in the fight for racial justice. In numerous pas-toral letters the bishops have called not only for social, educa-tional and economic equality of opportunity for black and white, but more recently also for full political equality. These demands have been repeatedly supported by political protests on the part of individual bishops and priests, especially in connection with the forced resettlement of non-white groups. The legality of the all-embracing apartheid legislation has been attacked by the bishops in the sharpest terms, but they have never fundamentally challenged the binding force of discriminatory laws. To that ex-tent the Catholic Church in South Africa works within the exist-ing system of domination, and has not so far, by boycott, civil disobedience or other forms of non-violent action, placed itself outside the racialist system.

Not so the Catholic bishops of Rhodesia.[11] Since the appearance in 1959 of the first pastoral letter by a Rhodesian bishop devoted to the racial question, the episcopate has deliberately discussed the political aspects of racialism. The move to political action came in 1970, when the leaders of the Catholic Church, together with the leadership of the Anglican and most of the Protestant Churches, announced that they were ending their collaboration with the government in primary education because of increased racial discrimination against the African population. In the same year sixteen Rhodesian Churches, under the leadership of the Catholic bishops, announced their intention to engage in civil disobedience. "We must obey God rather than men" (Acts 5. 29), said the Rhodesian bishops, and instructed church institutions to ignore a series of discriminatory constitutional measures. After a

[11] Cf. M. Traber, "Die katholische Kirche Rhodesiens in Widerstand", in Baumgartner, *op. cit.*, pp. 211 ff.

"tactical retreat" and partial compromise (February–November 1971), the bishops once more hardened their position. This must be the only case in modern Church history in which not just individual Christians but the whole of a country's episcopate have officially opposed the State with the threat of specific actions (civil resistance and non-co-operation). This political commitment is not shared, however, by the majority of white Catholics and by a minority of priests and nuns. For this reason the bishops are now concentrating on grass-roots politico-pastoral work in small groups.

The political commitment of the Church in southern Africa is at present a series of tentative steps rather than a programme which bears any relation to the reality of racial oppression. The intensification of this commitment is all the more urgent because racial discrimination in this area of the world is still justified as support for "Christian civilization".

Translated by Francis McDonagh

Bertrand De Clercq

Political Commitment and Liturgical Celebration

I. The Situation of the Question

SHOULD we have a "political" liturgy? For many who are directly concerned with the liturgy, it is primarily a practical question of trying to overcome on the one hand the lethargy of the people and on the other the gulf that exists between liturgy and life. For this reason, they attempt to bring the liturgy closer to the people by relating it more directly to contemporary life. A political liturgy is therefore one of the many experimental forms resulting from the same practical need to appeal to a wider group of Christians. Underlying this search for new effectiveness in liturgical expression is a new conception of the liturgy based on its secularization or desacralization. In its most extreme form, this results in a "Christianity without liturgy", which is, in turn, the consequence of faith without religion. This movement would seem, however, to be losing ground at present to a search for the transcendental or mystical element.

There may, however, be political reasons for making the liturgy political. It is difficult to avoid the impression that the current use of liturgy to propagate certain political attitudes or further certain political aims closely resembles its earlier use as a vehicle for a given ecclesiastical ideology. We should not forget, however, that, although there is always a risk of this, these political ends are not usually directly or exclusively politically inspired. Their ultimate inspiration is almost always religious. We may therefore say that the liturgy is used as a form of political commitment mediated through theology and can be regarded as a specific form of what has come to be called the "political relevance" of the Gospel and of Christian faith. This brings us inevitably to certain central weaknesses in the new political theology. Firstly, faced with real political facts, the term "political" has not yet been satisfactorily defined and, secondly, concrete imperatives and models[1] have not yet been provided by this theology.

Here, because of lack of space, I shall try to answer only one practical question. It is this. How can and must politically committed Christians give liturgical expression to that commitment? Although it is necessary to bridge the gulf between liturgy and life, what is most urgently required is not liturgical "effectiveness", but an adequate liturgical expression, in the local community of believers, of the political dimension of Christian life.

II. The Political and the Liturgical Dimensions

Both theologians and liturgists tend to make too few distinctions when they consider the political reality. It is useful in this context to observe the three fundamental but mutually related ambiguities which R. Aron has distinguished in our speaking about politics.[2]

Firstly, there is "policy"—the programme of action of a government, political party or group. This policy is almost always set in a framework of complex relationships of conflict, opposition and solidarity with other policies in the whole arena of "politics", in which the struggle for power and the whole process of decision making takes place. Secondly, there is a similar ambiguity in the term "history" between the event or process itself and our knowledge of it. In other words, we are all the object of the political process, but the explicit awareness that we have of it also forms an integral part of this process, which is, after all, a human activity. "The integration of man's political consciousness into the political reality raises the whole problem

---

[1] See, in connection with the liturgy, H. B. Meyer, *Politik im Gottesdienst?* (Innsbruck, 1971), pp. 68, 81.

[2] R. Aron, *Démocratie et totalitarisme* (Paris, 1965), pp. 21-6.

of the relationship between factual judgment (information) and value judgment (attitude)."[3] Thirdly, politics forms both a separate sector in society (political institutions, public functions, and so on) and one definite aspect of the whole of society. It is this that gives rise to the tension between the particular and the universal which is so characteristic of politics.

What has to be borne in mind is that the political contribution made to the liturgy by Christians will include, at least potentially, all these elements and that, as a result, this will be reflected in any attempt to make the liturgy more political. This in turn provides a good indication of the possibilities of the liturgy, its limitations and its diversity. I should like here to draw attention to a number of distinctions, the importance of which has been, in my view, to some extent underestimated in this particular context.

The liturgy is essentially a constitutive act. It is a real manifestation of the people of God in a particular place which thus represents the universal Church or makes it present in that place. In the Constitution on the Liturgy, 7, we read, for example, of the common *cultus publicus* that is carried out by the whole body of Christ, both head and members. This gives the liturgy a binding character and an official status in the Church which in turn impose certain limitations on man's freedom to experiment with or to change its form. A distinction, however, can and has to be made here between liturgy proper and paraliturgical "pious exercises" or "private devotions". Even though the latter are falling more and more into disuse, it would, in my opinion, be quite wrong to abandon the principle of paraliturgical practice altogether, because it provides a wide variety of possibilities for expressing the faith of a community in new and different forms. It hardly needs to be stressed, of course, that it is important to respect the special laws of every kind of liturgical action in order to allow full justice to be done to it in its own, particular way. As an example of this, the administration of a sacrament requires a different approach from a homily or from prayer said aloud by the whole community.

[3] *Op. cit.*, p. 24.

III. Political Interpretation and Religious Legitimation

We may certainly assume that any liturgical celebration will inevitably take place within a political context and that this context will not be without a religious significance. The first function of the liturgy, then, is that it should make those taking part in the celebration politically conscious precisely as Christians. The liturgical form will therefore be basically a provision of information together with a confrontation with the Gospel. An obvious and indeed inescapable model for all "political" liturgy is, of course, Dorothee Sölle's "political evening prayer of Cologne", despite or perhaps because of its clear exposure of the risks involved.

Let me refer briefly to one of these dangers. This experiment can be regarded as a form of paraliturgy which is not a cultic celebration and is directed towards a select and ecumenically "mixed" group of people. This is perhaps the greatest value of "political" liturgical experiments, but it is a very limited value, dangerous in that it can be regarded as the only valid form of liturgy today. It may even come to replace the eucharistic or sacramental liturgy, with the possible consequence that little or no attempt may be made to do justice to the legitimate "political" aspect of the eucharistic liturgy itself.

This political aspect is in fact brought out in the "protest masses" that have been celebrated for some years now in various parts of South America. The express intention of these eucharistic celebrations is to make those present conscious of their oppressed state. "Every truthful and consciously celebrated Eucharist can be regarded as the most radical . . . act of protest", proclaiming and making present the rule of Christ, "the only saviour and liberator, the only Lord of history and of man". This implies that "his rule excludes every other rule which seeks to dominate men and that in him all men are made free. . . . By celebrating the Eucharist, we commit ourselves to the work of removing all forms of political, social and ideological oppression that are incompatible with what we have proclaimed."[4]

In a situation of political oppression, the liturgy becomes what

[4] S. Galilea, "Les messes de protestation", in *Parole et Mission*, 14 (1971), p. 334.

J. Bishop has called a "subversive activity", which, although it does not in itself raise any serious controversial political questions, undoubtedly has political consequences. These are not always prominent, but, in the situation of Latin America, the political interpretation of the Eucharist is usually that "the Christians who take part in the celebration are aware of what they are really proclaiming in the liturgy".[5]

In both these examples, the concrete way in which political consciousness is given the form of a political attitude is open to criticism. The "political evening prayer" has been criticized because it makes a one-sided choice of biblical texts and interprets them in a one-sided way, preaches in an aggressive tone and manipulates the public in an authoritarian manner.[6] In a word, it uses prayer and the proclamation of the Gospel as a political weapon. The choice of Bible readings, homilies and prayers of petition in my second example, the "protest masses", is also aggressive. It is not really possible to say that this way of forming political consciousness is inherent in "political" liturgy. We can, however, say with reasonable certainty that there is always a risk in this type of liturgy that the essence of prayer and worship will be lost in political manifestation and that faith will sink to the level of ideology.

It is important to cling to the basic principle that Christians come together primarily to give a liturgical form to their shared faith. There are, of course, cases of Christians being already united by a common political aim, but, even if this political unity has an explicitly Christian motivation, it cannot always be given an adequate liturgical form. To create a "political" liturgy in such cases may simply be to insert politics into a liturgical framework and to further a political aim with the help of religion.[7] Man's worship of God and his confession of Christ have a special political relevance, but not as a confirmation of a political attitude. They are politically relevant above all as a confrontation

---

[5] *Op. cit.*, p. 335.
[6] See, for example, P. Cornehl, "Öffentlicher Gottesdienst", in P. Cornehl and H.-E. Bahr, eds., *Gottesdienst und Öffenlichkeit* (Hamburg, 1970), pp. 183 and 189 ff.
[7] It is possible to imagine liturgical assemblies of members of a Christian political party held with the purpose of strengthening "political" faith and setting a liturgical seal on political convictions!

between politics and faith. Any attempt to make the liturgy political must, I am convinced, always be based on this confrontation.

IV. CRITICISM OF SOCIETY AND SELF-CRITICISM

The attendance at the average liturgical celebration will reflect the situation in the whole of society—that of political pluralism. This is the most difficult problem facing anyone conscious of the need to give liturgical expression to this confrontation between politics and faith.

Above all, it is necessary to ensure that a *communio fidelium*, a unity in faith, is brought to bear, within any liturgical celebration, on the contemporary social and political phenomenon of pluralism in convictions, values, interests and aims. This unity in faith is often placed at a higher level than all political divisions, but this becomes problematical as soon as we try to give it a political relevance. Many examples in the past and the present have shown that there is a tendency to think of this unity in faith as something previously given or obligatory, leading inevitably either to a religiously imposed political unity which is in reality only a Christian partiality or else to a call to reconcile all political differences in a "higher" unity which is merely abstract. This is fundamentally the dilemma in which all politically relevant liturgy find itself. Either it is a preaching of universal brotherly love which steers clear of all debate and avoids taking sides or else it preaches one or other course of political action.[8] Even in its present form, the so-called Christian criticism of society, a politically relevant liturgy may simply avoid repeating or reformulating principles supported by more or less everyone and criticisms opposed by more or less everyone by being politically committed on one side or the other in the case of concrete, local problems.

How can this situation be avoided? I think the political struggle must be openly and explicitly involved in the liturgy. At the same time, Christian unity must be seen as a unity of believers, that is, of people who are involved in conflict and are yet trying to express their conviction that unity can eventually be

[8] J. Guichard, "Options politiques de l'Eglise", *Lumière et Vie*, 20 (1971), pp. 76–81.

attained as the end result of this conflict. I would therefore be in favour of a liturgy that is politically partial. At the same time, this liturgy ought to be relative in its expression, above all appealing always to the freedom of those taking part. It should also be possible for part of this liturgy to consist of a discussion of political points of view, so long as there is a strict adherence to the principle that those representing each side in this political debate make their religious motivation clear and are ready to pray together.

As far as this liturgical prayer is concerned, self-criticism plays an essential part. This is fundamentally the expression of man's imperfection and his affirmation of hope that God is always present in the political struggle as a power of reconciliation. "In prayer, man expresses himself in the presence of God. He expresses his sorrow about the Kingdom of God that is still absent, and his hope that this Kingdom will come."[9] This involves complaints and accusations, but it has a further dimension—"The Church will accept all the private and social longings of mankind and produce them in the confrontation with the images of the future contained in the biblical promises. In opposition to all cynicism and fatalism, the Church will also try to throw light on all that we have to be thankful for."[10]

Translated by David Smith

[9] D. Sölle and F. Steffensky, eds., *Politisches Nachtgebet in Köln* (Stuttgart, 2nd edn., 1969), p. 23.
[10] P. Cornehl, *op. cit.*, p. 181.

Normann Hepp

The Christian Community and Community Work

I. COMMUNITY WORK

SOCIAL work can deal with individuals, with groups and with a whole community (village, part of a town, town, region). Correspondingly, three methods of social work have been developed in theory and practice: individual, group and community work. Community work,[1] the third and youngest discipline of social work, starts from the premise that the most important social problems cannot be solved simply by plans and measures imposed "from above". In order to create humane and just living conditions in work and free time, the community, that is the broad mass of the population, should learn to formulate its own interests and needs and carry them through politically.

It is the community worker's task to advise the people how to sort out their problems and support them in finding an independent, communal solution: to help the community help itself. To enable the community to take political action in this way is itself a political act.

---

[1] See, for example, J. Boer and K. Utermann, *Gemeinwesenarbeit* (Stuttgart, 1971); R. H. Hauser, *Die kommende Gesellschaft* (Munich, 1971); N. Hepp, ed., *Neue Gemeindemodelle* (Vienna, 1971); C. W. Müller and P. Nimmermann, *Stadtplanung und Gemeinwesenarbeit* (Munich, 1971); M. G. Ross, *Gemeinwesenarbeit* (Freiburg, 1968); L. E. Schaller, *Kirche und Gemeinwesenarbeit—Konflikt und Versöhnung* (Gelnhausen, 1972); W. Schneider, *Aktion Gemeinde heute* (Wuppertal, 1970).

The action which is envisaged by community work to increase
effective participation takes place under different titles according
to those responsible and the type of problem in hand: as community work through welfare societies, clubs and foundations,
for instance in areas where many are homeless or there is a lot
of new building; as public works and popular participation
through the planning authorities in the cleaning up of older
quarters of a town and the planning of areas of new building;
work through political groups in different districts of a town;
initiatives by ordinary people, often in oddly assorted groups, in
cases of hardship when they arise; help for developing countries.
On closer inspection two conceptions can be differentiated, one
more harmonizing and one more conflict-orientated. Community
work has a mainly harmonizing effect, where it stops up the
gaps in public assistance, helps existing institutions in co-ordin-
ating their work or by means of a certain right of consultation
introduces people's representatives into the planning bodies. Conflict-orientated, aggressive community work is found in some
popular initiatives, particularly when a minority, in terms of
numbers and power, succeeds in pressing its interests; similarly
in left-wing work (for instance, Black Power, communist parties),
where the aim is not to improve the existing social system, but to
overthrow it. A midway position between these is offered in the
widely-read textbook by Ross. According to him community
work can be defined as a process through which a community
establishes its needs and goals, arranges them in order of priority,
develops the confidence and the will to set to work, finds out
methods and sources of help to enable it to do so, proceeds to
action, and in order to do this encourages co-operative work and
the capacity of the community for self-help.

Community work, developed in North America and in the
Netherlands, is today a proper subject for educational training
probably in most Western countries. Because of the very various
socio-political and ideological points of view there is no unified
theory and practice. Common to all conceptions is, however, the
enlisting of sociological methods and principles in an attempt
to enable a community to solve its problems (in whatever way
these may be seen) by means of self-help.

II. Have Christian Communities and Community Work anything fundamental in common?

1. *Interpretations of the Christian Message of Salvation*

It is the Church's mission to mediate salvation, that is, to make it possible. But *in what* does this salvation which is to be mediated lie? Simply in consoling or in providing a meaning in situations of disaster or crisis in human life? Or in living in a community that simply compensates for social disadvantages? Or is the socially conditioned nature of individual ills recognized and not only the treatment of the symptoms but also the fight against the causes of such evils counted as part of the Church's work of salvation?

For whom is salvation to be made possible? Only for members of the Christian community? Or salvation for all? Then let the Church make the concerns of the community, and in particular the fringe groups, into its concerns—the Church for the community!

Through whom should this happen? Through those in authority as part of their job? Or does the community understand its role as an instrument of the diaconate and try to enable the afflicted to help themselves, to turn to political action in a Christian spirit?

2. *Theology and Community Work*

If the Church understands its service to the world as a critical collaboration, guided by the Gospel, in the building up of a humane and just community and if the community sees its task as analysing the socially conditioned circumstances of all people, measuring them against the demands of the Gospel, and working together with those afflicted and also with non-Christian forces to improve them, then the Church will want to join in community work. In this work the Church will make use of the statistical findings of community work, without adopting its aims uncritically. Community work presupposes then a theology which is capable of playing the role of a praxis norm for church action, for community work at the parish level.

III. How can the Christian Communities learn to recognize their Mission in Community Work?

1. *First Experiences*

(a) *The Parishes*

Whether an attempt to equip our parishes for their service to the community will be successful is problematic. The poll of representatives on the occasion of the Catholic Synod in the Federal Republic of Germany showed in its results that any increase in piety led to a decrease in discernment of any need to improve our social system and the other way round. In the student parishes the debate with Marxism has caused the formation of a strong socio-critical consciousness. On account of the exceptional situation of these parishes, however, no Church community work worth mentioning has developed and equally the effect on Church praxis has been small.

Only in very few territorial parishes are there positive experiences;[2] however, the integration of parish and committed groups, of theology and social action has not been successful in every case.

(b) *The Appointment of Community Workers*

In recent years in the Federal Republic, social workers have been appointed in some local parishes, after having been trained in community work. According to the mostly unpublished reports I have seen,[3] these experiments have failed. Within one or two years there were resignations. The following reasons for failure were mentioned:

(1) A vague *theological understanding* of its role on the part of the Church: whose Church is it? Is it a community which has mainly to look after its own members and the smooth functioning of its own organization or is it open to all? This was found to

---

[2] See, for example, Don Enzo Mazzi, "Die Gemeinde im Isolotto", and R. Delaney, "Die Pfarrgemeinde San Miguelito", in Normann Hepp, *Neue Gemeindemodelle* (Vienna, 1971); *Gemeindeaufbau und Gemeinwesenarbeit*, volume I, *Bilanz 71 der Evangelischen Gemeinde Heerstrasse Nord, Berlin* (Gelnhausen, 1972).

[3] Martin Schofer, "Evangelische Gemeinde Freiburg-Landwasser", in Normann Hepp, *op. cit.* In this section (III 1b), I have used, sometimes word for word, a report by Werner Ehinger of Freiburg.

be the basic problem, particularly when it was a question of ecumenism, collaboration and the role of the laity, of social work with fringe groups or sacrifices for the community in general without any advantage for the Church.

(2) *Conflict of roles* between parish priest and community worker—power must be divided. This loss of power and prestige is a great personal problem for the priest, in addition to the uncertainty about roles which is general.

(3) *Unclear role of the social worker*—the ideas of the social worker, the priest and the groups in the community are often widely divergent. Frequently the social worker is overwhelmed by innumerable individual items requiring attention, so that he has neither time nor energy to act as a stimulus for members of the community or groups or initiate courses of action in the spirit of community work.

(4) *Vagueness about Church community work*: Quite apart from the fact that there are various directions for community work in general, the expectations of Church community work are very various, but often exalted and usually false, particularly when it is understood as a method by which the community ship can be piloted through the rocky waters of the secular world without worrying the passengers.

Besides this the experiences of Church community work are rarely evaluated and used fruitfully in training and praxis. This means that social workers are in general little prepared for the parish situation and the methods necessary there, as well as the theological argumentation and motivation; on the other side, the theologians meet the social sciences with lack of understanding, nervousness, or else an obvious feeling of superiority.

The following *conclusions*, to be used for work on new models, were drawn from these failed experiments:

(1) *The appointment* of the community worker not to the parish as previously, but at an intermediate level. This means greater freedom vis-à-vis the parish authorities, but also the danger on both sides of isolation, so that the community work is no longer done by Christian communities guided by theology and the communities themselves avoid their duties in the social sphere.

(2) *Expert sociological and theological consultation on the models.* A prerequisite for this is that it should be financed by the diocese and should be in collaboration with experts in universities and colleges for the social sciences.

(c) *Collaboration with Others engaged in Community Work*

In view of the self-sufficiency of the average parish it is perhaps not surprising that examples of ecumenical co-operation are scarcely to be found.

Where co-operation with non-Christian workers is concerned, the picture is even worse, even where the employers are in part Church institutions. The parishes, or rather their leaders, keep their distance mostly on theological grounds. Behind this is often an inner uncertainty vis-à-vis the hard, in many ways unsympathetic criticism of the mainly Marxist arguments of the social workers. On account of their negative experiences with the Church, strengthened by the negative value put on the social role of the Church even in lay theological circles, they have no hopes that the parishes might become partners in dialogue and action to improve living conditions. Lacking both patience and competence for theological argumentation, they cannot communicate their awareness of the problem nor their concern to the parishes. So these then tend to confirm them in their isolated position.

Collaboration with workers outside the parish is, however, absolutely necessary for the Church community work, if it wants to be both just and effective.

2. *The Church's Opportunities for Action in the Community*

In order to plan the Church's way forward it is essential to take stock, making a real assessment, and then to mobilize, after due consideration, the entire range of opportunities for action which the Church has at its disposal.

(a) *The Parishes*

In the average parish, there are a number of more problem-orientated work-parties and groups, a many stranded net available for action between individuals and groups. As the results of the poll showed, a by no means small section of outsiders declared themselves ready for commitment within the Church. In addition to these there are the not inconsiderable number of people employed full-time in the service of the parish.

The Sunday services are still probably the numerically strongest regular meetings of inhabitants in any community (even when, as for example in Munich, only 10% of Catholics attend church). To this quantitative finding must be added the qualitative significance and effect of public worship and also of the Church's participation in communal inaugural or dedication ceremonies and special events on individuals and on the community, without this needing to be conscious in any way. For the most part the spheres of Church educational and social work have become separate from the parish.

(b) *Educational Work*

The opportunity for Christian communities to have considerable influence on the community as a whole lies in their nursery school work. Eighty-six per cent of nursery schools in the Federal Republic are run by the churches. In the schools, religious education is in a state of severe crisis, which can only be properly resolved if the teachers are empowered to make their contribution to a more humane and just control and organization of life from a Christian point of view in accordance with the educational programme in the schools. This also points in the direction of social work. Much the same is true of the chances offered the Church by its youth work and adult education at a parish level or beyond or outside the parish.

Through their work in education, the churches have a regular, sometimes profound, influence on a large proportion of all children between three and six, and all school children. In addition, they influence a percentage of young people and adults, which varies according to circumstances, through educational work outside schools.

Further, they have opportunities in the field of professional training and through the mass media.

(c) *Social Work*

Almost invariably separate from the parishes is the work of various social organizations supported by the Church. The variety of specialized counselling and Caritas centres, both on a local and a regional basis, is steadily increasing. The number of itinerant helpers, homes, institutions, hospitals, schools and workshops with a great diversity of purposes, and training centres ranging right up to higher education centres for social studies, is impossible to estimate.

(d) *Summary*

Among all the institutions independent of the State, it is the churches which have the richest opportunities locally for community work and the means of carrying it out. Whether they apply these means in the most appropriate way, indeed whether they are even able to inspire them with a Christian spirit, is another question.

This is particularly true of organizations in the field of social work and education, which have relieved the parishes of tasks which were originally their responsibility, but which, by so doing, have contributed to the impoverishment of the parish as an institution. Parishes have thus lost an important function and have become remote from human problems. On the other hand, this development has made it more difficult for these two areas to maintain a basis of faith and theology. The parish, once relieved of these original responsibilities, is no longer obliged to develop a theology as a basis for action. It is no wonder that for members of a younger generation confronting the problems of social work, Marxist principles have increasingly come to fill out this theological gap, even in professional training centres run by the Church.

Consequently everything depends on whether the Church, in its local situation, applies that power which it actually possesses in social communities for the good of those communities and in a Christian spirit: that is, whether it deliberately commits itself to community work. If it is no longer able to do that, it has no right to these influential means which it possesses.

3. *Some Points with regard to Methods*

The methods of community work in general as laid down in handbooks apply also to community work done by the Church. In addition, the following points are relevant specifically for Church community work.

(a) *Interdisciplinary Co-operation*

When Church activity in the field of social work is considered, the already established social and educational organizations are usually left out of account, either unconsciously or explicitly on the grounds that they are supposedly independent organizations. This is a disastrous mistake. The strength of the Church lies precisely in the wide range of its possibilities for action.

Genuine co-operation would have to function something like this. Local experts in social work must present an account and an analysis of the social problems in the community to the parishes; the latter would then have to compare the situations described with the message of the Gospel and, using the educational institutions at the Church's disposal, try to bring about a broad *communal awareness* of the problems and try to *promote activity* to improve the conditions. Such co-operation is also necessary for help in *integration work* (ghettos) and for the undertaking of *preventive measures* in social and educational work.

The Church would have great opportunities, as yet unrealized, in developing interdisciplinary *models*, which could be exemplary for the whole community.

(b) *The Importance of Church Services for Social Work*

The failures of attempts at community work at parish level, referred to above, were made inevitable by the fact that the socially committed community leader of such parish work, or the groups and helpers involved, were denied a share in church services.

Church leaders, with their acute sense of power structures, know that social commitment within the parish will bring no fundamental alterations unless it is seriously related to church services.

Parish community work is only possible in connection with church services: by this means the activities of parish groups are turned into official matters of concern of the parish; by the confrontation of social problems with faith, the social commitment of the worshipping community is challenged, as well as the "real" ground of faith of the community, which is generally regarded as being separate from social work and politics.

Worship which influences the social work of the parish gives to it an official character and also the motivating power of faith.

(c) *Starting-Points*

There are all kinds of starting-points which can lead to community work in the parishes. If resignation and radicalization are both to be avoided, parishes will have to prepare themselves for a *slow* process of emancipation. For this reason, they should start by setting themselves limited objectives which will provide for a sense of achievement. In the long term satisfaction in the work itself is more important than the lightning solution of the problems.

A few starting-points may be listed here: demands for adequate public facilities in the community, such as nursery schools, schools, playgrounds, youth centres, provision for old people; a share in town planning, especially in areas of new development and resettlement. In such cases confrontations with political institutions and parties are almost inevitable, and this will provide opportunity for the developing and establishing of Christian policies and their basic outlines.

Children's play centres have been built up by numerous parents' groups on their own initiative and at their own expense; Christian communities could bring the same measure of commitment to their own nursery schools. Pre-school education should be thought of particularly in its compensatory function for children from disadvantaged homes. In this connection it should be possible to make a wider range of parents aware of the present limited aims of *schooling*, which for socially conditioned reasons have become one-sided and achievement-oriented. Further starting-points are: problems in education, conditions of work, use of leisure, and the problems of disadvantaged groups such as old people, the handicapped, released prisoners, foreign workers, the inmates of homes and institutions, etc.

(4) *The Umkirch Model*

(a) *Basic Propositions*

The aim is to enable the parish to become aware of its responsibilities in the community, to improve living conditions and to understand this as the fulfilment of the mission of salvation. Individual seminars and programmes of action enable limited objectives in this larger plan to be attained—learning by doing.

The integration of educational, social and parish work puts an end to purely academic educational work, to purely activistic social work and to parish work which is remote from contemporary problems.

All forms of work are used and purposefully integrated: lectures with discussions, house visits to promote interest and awareness, parties, worship, political action.

(b) *Method*

(1) An initiative group from the parish (the parish priest should work with it) chooses a social problem in the community and plans a seminar.

(2) On the first evening, at a plenary session, a speaker introduces the topic, for example, "Children in our country today" or "Old People". The important thing here is that the social background of existing problems should be explained and the desire to improve them should be aroused.

(3) Working parties are formed during the second half of the evening. These will work according to concrete suggestions, finding out about the local situation (collecting information about existing institutions, mobilizing both the "victims" and the "responsible authorities" by their enquiries).

(4) The results of enquiries and proposals for improvements are then, two to three weeks later, presented by the working parties at a second plenary evening. The information collected is handed on to all present, views are worked out about a programme of priorities, and

(5) a church service is planned, in which—wherever possible together with the "victims"—the problems and the proposals for action are presented together with their theological basis (discussion either during or after the service).

(6) The formation of a permanent working party, which takes charge of the problem, inaugurates the necessary courses of action, where appropriate with other groups, and reports back frequently in the course of church services.

A more detailed description of the "Umkirch model" and a report on the first attempts will be published shortly. Methods of social work are therefore a help for the Christian community, in so far as these communities are prepared to shoulder that political responsibility for society which the Gospel lays down: to act as the resources of a Church for the world.

Translated by Rosaleen Ockenden

PART II
DOCUMENTATION
CONCILIUM

Klemens Richter

The Political Commitment of the Christian Community in East Germany

THE German Democratic Republic is in practice a state with an undeniably authoritarian and atheistic view of life. Consequently the question of the Christian community's political commitment can scarcely be adequately considered without some explanation of the political situation, as it effects both society and the Church. The Evangelical Church had to come to terms years ago at all levels, both theologically and pragmatically, with the problem of Christian commitment in a socialist system. There were many reasons for this. There are 10 million Evangelical Christians as against 1·3 million Catholics in a population of 17 million. Pressure from the State is stronger and there is greater decentralization of Church leadership. There are theological faculties at the otherwise atheistic universities, and so on. The Catholic hierarchy, on the other hand, concentrates on pastoral work in the narrow sense and tries to preserve at the same time a wide-ranging neutrality in the entire political sphere. The individual communities are all the more willing to follow the bishops in this attitude, because the parties and mass organizations, in particular the CDU in the Democratic Republic with the monthly *Begegnung* (*Encounter*, a periodical for progressive Catholics, 12th year), understand by the political commitment of the community exclusively a clear adherence to socialist social policy on the one hand and to the State's foreign policy on the other.

A community commitment that would, for instance, take the initiatives of the newer political theology as the theory for its action, is rejected by the SED leadership as Western theology and therefore unsuitable for the establishment of socialism. Thus, as recently as 1971, P. Verner, a member of the Politbüro and secretary of the central committee of the Party, explained that the communists had no intention of "interfering in the theological affairs of the churches", but that the Church "cannot take up a position betweeen the capitalist and socialist camps nor one at a 'critical distance' to our existing state". And to G. Götting, chairman of the CDU and president of Parliament, it was self-evident that "in theology and in the Church the overthrow of all ideologies, which in the circumstances are useful to imperialism, is an unalterable prerequisite for any effective processes of conscious re-orientation" and that a "firm attempt to distinguish all the theologically disguised variants of neo-bourgeois ideology" was essential.

In view of this it is understandable that the bishops do not welcome, and certainly do not advocate, any political commitment of the community that goes beyond purely charitable work. The efforts of student groups in particular and of an admittedly rather small group of academics and priests to work towards more socio-political commitment is opposed by the ecclesiastical establishment. As far as the Democratic Republic is concerned, it is certainly possible to speak of a Church dominated by the clergy. The unity of clergy and laity, in many ways welcome, is in this case the unity of a monologue which acts as a brake on any activities. In the view of W. Trilling, an Oratorian from Leipzig, the main aim up until now, that of preserving the *status quo*, has been purchased at a price, that of "the danger of the ghetto mentality, of life in an enclave, of comfort in the warmth of the Catholic nest. We know, however, from experience as well as from doctrine, that Christianity can only remain alive when it bears witness, when it sees work and does it, when it serves and in serving finds and fulfils itself." There is no dialogue with the socialist environment. The mentality of two opposing camps predominates in spite of an officially more relaxed atmosphere.

The dilemma in which the communities find themselves between the demand for political commitment, not only from the State but also here and there from inside the Church, and the existing ghetto mentality is clear from the introductory paper

"The Apostolate and Service to the World" for the pastoral synod beginning in 1973 in the Democratic Republic, the first national synod to be held in a socialist state. Any possible community commitment is circumscribed in fundamental statements such as these: "The Church cannot endorse the ideological basis of the State and those provisions of the State which result from it"; "It is difficult to make any general rule about a limit to co-operation in social work. But this limit is certainly overstepped when the Christian is asked to give up responsible, relevant action and act against his conscience"; "However much Christians must oppose the establishment of an atheistic ideology, they are trying, none the less, to co-operate in the realization of humanitarian aims"; "Work in the social field is not devoid of risk for the Christian. Conflict situations arise which present the individual with questions of conscience to decide"; "Christians who are discriminated against because of their work for peace should be able to rely on the support of the Church". Such statements, which circumscribe Christian commitment at any rate initially and which maintain a due critical distance, find no endorsement on the part of the State. "A critical distance" is here misunderstood as opposition, which the SED will not allow. For *Begegnung* (1972, Heft 6, p. 5) therefore, "the path pointed out in the introductory papers is not a path into the future. It leads not to the requisite service to the world, but to isolation—which can only damage the Church."

This biased attitude of those in positions of responsibility in the Democratic Republic towards any political commitment of the community inevitably leads to a decrease in political activity in the communities. The dominance of the ghetto mentality means that the Christian community excites little notice and gives little offence in society. This renunciation of a public role does not, however, prevent demands for such a commitment being made in the particularly open-minded atmosphere of the student community and academic circles. Ever since Walter Ulbricht, Chairman of the Council of State, explained that "there is no conflict between Christianity and the humanist goals of socialism", the decrease in crude atheistic propaganda and anti-Church politics has meant that the earlier strong feeling that a practising Christian was only a second-class citizen is gradually disappearing. Various ameliorations in the Church-State relationship have put in question the exclusively defensive mentality, in particular as far as intellectuals are concerned. (Although, independently of this, it is for example more difficult for a Christian to obtain higher education.)

Many, on the other hand, are anxious to leave their self-imposed ghetto and actively desire a confrontation with their environment. They are looking for a Christian way of life within their political system. Until 1966 there were no public comments from communities on the subject of political commitment. Then an action group of priests and laymen from Halle (like common-purpose groups in the West) made the following criticism: "If we persist with this hopeless lack of perspective, we have no chance of being taken seriously as a responsible partner by the State or even of being heard when it is a question of evaluating morally vital pronouncements made by the State or intervening decisively where moral norms are being transgressed in unprecedented fashion." And elsewhere they noted: "If we believe that the obligation to commitment in public and national life is a Christian obligation in our situation too, then a recognition of the political authority of the German Democratic Republic is the sole starting-point which can make possible a collaboration, in which criticism and admonition are not suspect from the outset."

For this circle of communities, and also for a minority of Christians in other communities, it did and does not need to be stressed that "in the face of the omnipresence of state totalitarianism", collaboration is only possible "where decisions cannot be thrust down our throats in advance. . . . We need in fact to have scope in which the freedom to make the appropriate decisions is guaranteed to us" (duplicated correspondence). The vast majority of communities and the hierarchy are, however, of the opinion that there is insufficient scope for this.

In contrast with this view, a growing minority is convinced that it is possible for Christians to collaborate without having to fulfil all the State's preconceptions about political commitment by the community. These Christians ask how they should use the opportunity, given to them at the parents' advisory boards, of breaking the totalitarian claims of the State in the sphere of culture and education? Ought it not to be possible, within the trade-union framework, to subject the increasing hardships in the social conditions of the employed to fair and appropriate examination and redress? "If we can succeed in working together with the communists and civil servants on these and similar bodies on the basis of what is right and proper and of mutual respect . . . , then we shall have fulfilled something of our call to commitment."

The view which we see forming here stems from the premise that such areas of free decision can only be opened up through active commitment. To have a community which continues to reject its environment is sure to be pleasant for the state system, for it possesses no attraction for its environment, it "dies out" and even gives support to a dogmatic communism. Development by-passes such a community and it no longer really lives. The complaint often voiced, that any political collaboration seems to support all the unjust actions of the State, too, is rejected by those who favour such commitment, since they contend that it is precisely through this collaboration of Christians that the totality of the state is broken, the totality which is at the root of all the violation of moral standards.

None the less they are aware that the collaboration of Christians cannot be motivated by the possible success: "The cross is our symbol in all such activity; and precisely here can the experience of the cross serve us well, in the State's misuse of our intervention for propaganda purposes, also in the misunderstandings we arouse in our fellow Christians and in the suspicions which grow from these. The signs of the times which speak for our work and the experience of the cross are what encourage us to follow the way of Christian commitment in the German Democratic Republic."

This is, of course, far from being a description of models for political commitment in the Christian community in the GDR. But definite models of this sort, which are perhaps practised by communities in some places, are frankly impossible in the circumstances described above, in the face of the very different preconceptions of hierarchy and party. In addition, the fixation with the society of the Federal Republic of West Germany was far too deeply rooted in the consciousness of most of the faithful. In its fetishism for the West, the Church often presents the spectacle of an agonized struggle with seemingly antiquated traditions. It is only gradually that new forms evolve under this crust of traditions. The group, the intimate circle, becomes the focal point. Bound up with this is a strong neighbourhood service; for instance, there are young married couples, like those in a Dresden parish, who meet regularly for discussion and mutual help and who are looking for ways to engage their circle politically. Here and there such spontaneous groups evolve, in which Christians and non-Christians associate at a human level, free from thoughts of career, from loneliness and anonymity, who understand one another not as enemies but as members of their socialist society.

In addition to the charitable work of individual members of the community (for example, voluntary work in hospital, work of reparation, and so on), there are occasions for the whole community to involve itself in public work, where this is non-controversial, for instance, the provision of amenities for the whole community (such as children's playgrounds, etc.) or help in disasters. Comments on socio-political happenings are problematic, since any criticism by the whole community would be misunderstood as organized protest. Up until now, this has been dangerous for anyone except the bishops, who have been able to express their opinion on such subjects as marriage and family legislation, abortion and the socialist youth dedication ceremony (a substitute for Christian confirmation) in pastoral letters and petitions.

Definite models for political commitment, which neither persist in running on traditional lines nor lapse into pure approbation of the State's actions, can only develop within the East German Catholic communities if the reality of the existing social environment is neither rejected as hostile nor simply accepted apathetically or with resignation. It is chiefly on this basis that there are possibilities of Christian collaboration in neighbourhood groups and trade unions, divorce and conflict commissions, etc. A Christianity entirely thrown back on the cultic Church, such as has been largely true until today, has no chance of survival in this socialist system. The Protestant evangelical community recognized this long ago.

Translated by Rosaleen Ockenden

Hermann Janssen

The Political Commitment of the Christian Communities in Papua, New Guinea

IN ANY examination of political commitment in Papua, New Guinea, the interplay of socio-political and religious forces with regard to socio-economic welfare is of particular importance for the Christian communities. Our aim here is to demonstrate this interplay (configuration) in four community models. These are pre-Christian, early Christian, syncretisitic and local communities. "Political commitment" is understood in this contribution in its wider sense as public and social spheres of influence.

There is an almost complete lack of critical, historical and empirical research into the Church in Papua, New Guinea. This essay should therefore be regarded only as a preliminary attempt at an anthropological and sociological analysis and a pastoral and theological evaluation. This article is based partly on the studies indicated below,[1] but for the most part on personal research material.

[1] The following books and articles are relevant to my article. I. *Source and information material*: R. H. Condrington, *The Melanesians. Studies in their Anthropology and Folk-lore* (Oxford, 1891); G. Brown, *Melanesians and Polynesians. Their life-histories described and compared* (London, 1910); B. Malinowski, *Argonauts of the Western Pacific. An Account of Native Enterprise and Adventure in the Archipelagoes of Melanesian New Guinea* (London, 1922); M. Mead, *New Lives for Old: Cultural Transformation-Manus, 1928–1953* (London, 1956); P. Lawrence, *Road Belong Cargo. A Study of the Cargo Movement in the Southern Madang District, New Guinea* (Melbourne, 1964); P. Lawrence and M. J. Meggitt, *Gods, Ghosts and Men in Melanesia. Some Religions of Australian New Guinea and the New Hebrides* (Melbourne, 1965); C. D. Rowley, *The New Guinea Villager. A Retrospect from 1964* (Melbourne, 1965); A. R.

I. Pre-Christian Communities

In Papua, New Guinea (excluding West Irian or Indonesian New Guinea), there are today roughly 2·4 million inhabitants. This population is split up into more than 700 language groups, that is at least 700 social groups, which divide racially into Melanesians (coastal areas and islands) and Papuans (highlands and interior). Although these societies show marked differences in their social structure, they none the less show surprisingly similar patterns in their communal and religious attitudes.

The model for the pre-Christian or traditional communities of Papua can be briefly sketched as follows: Society, organized in complicated and relatively small communities (extended families, tribes and alliances of tribes) and based on real or imagined blood relationship and marriage, has to maintain itself by a constant internal and external power struggle.

In the internal power struggle the group elders ("big men" not "chiefs") climb up and down the political ladder. In the external power struggle, the group gains or loses influence over neighbouring groups. The internal and external political power relationships are in this way far from stagnating; they are, in fact, extraordinarily dynamic.

Political power is based on social wealth (many wives and

Tippett, *Solomon Islands Christianity. A Study of Growth and Obstruction* (World Studies of Churches in Mission, London, 1967); F. Steinbauer, *Melanesische Cargo-Kulte. Neureligiöse Heilsbewegungen in der Südsee* (Munich, 1971); W. von Krause, *Junges Neuguinea. Ein Informationsbuch* (Neuendelsau, n.d.). II. *Articles and analyses*: P. Lawrence, "Cargo Thinking as a Future Political Force in Papua and New Guinea", *The Journal of the Papua and New Guinea Society* (Port Moresby), 1 (1966–1967), 1, pp. 20–24. P. Lawrence, "Politics and 'True Knowledge' ", *New Guinea* (Sydney), 2 (1967), 1, pp. 34–49. P. Chatterton, "The Missionaries, Working themselves out of a Job", *New Guinea*, 3 (1968), 1, pp. 12–18. H. Janssen, "Mid-Course Correction, The Role of the Church in Melanesia", *Catalyst* (Goroka), 1 (1971), 2, pp. 5–23. P. Murphy, "In the Light of History, From Mission in New Guinea to Church of New Guinea", *Catalyst* 1 (1971), 2, pp. 4–31. J. Snyders, "The Best of Two Worlds, Functional Substitutes and Christian Secularity", *Catalyst*, 1 (1971), 2, pp. 47–60. J. Momis, "The Super Clan, Church Unity in Melanesia", *Catalyst*, 1 (1971), 4, pp. 4–8. H. Janssen, "Religion and Secularization, Pacific Cultures, Christianity and Development", *Catalyst* 2 (1971), 2, pp. 50–68. "Melanesian Institute, The Church as Local community", *Catalyst*, Special Edition, 1 (1972).

many trading partners), on economic potential (pigs, money from mussels, local husbandry and prestige-winning feasts for the barter of goods), as well as on ritual knowledge ("true knowledge") that has been handed down from their ancestors and that has to be safeguarded by feasts of masks and dance ("singsing"), as well as by sacrificial ceremonies (pig sacrifice).

The group with their elders is concerned to guarantee their social and economic welfare by their communal method of work and, more especially, by the cult of their dead and ancestor worship. In this desire for social and economic security primitive technology and economy consciously play a far smaller part than socio-religious ritual. The Papuans, however, lay more emphasis on a political and economic pragmatism, whereas the Melanesians are ritual pragmatists.

To sum up and simplify we might perhaps say that the politically minded community in the traditional society of Papua is above all religious in outlook. It tries constantly to activate this consciousness in communal and religious rites, in order to safeguard its socio-economic welfare. This religious and yet pragmatic mentality is characterized as "cargoism", that is, an ideology based on goods or cargo.

II. Early Christian Communities

The Christian mission in Papua started shortly before the turn of the century. More or less by the beginning of the Second World War, the coastal areas and islands belonged almost entirely to one of the bigger Christian Churches (Catholic, Lutheran, Methodist, Anglican). Missionary work in the highlands and interior began in about 1930 and has still not ended today; it shows a far greater fragmentation in the commitment of the bigger Churches and of the many small sects. In some districts there are even rivalries between the missionary Churches. Today almost 60% of the population belong to Christian Churches; about half of these are Catholic Christians.

The main objective of early Christian missionary work in Papua is twofold: the saving of souls and the civilizing of the people. This motivation is reflected also in the methods of the missions, which were expressed on the one hand in the catechumenate and the administration of the sacraments and sacramentals, and on the other hand in schools, hospitals and plantations. The civilizing motivation is frequently coupled with the spiritual objective, in so far as educational, medical and economic aids are not infrequently seen as a means to an end. It seems that the motivation for conversion, that is for turning to Christianity, on the part of the Melanesians and Papuans is mainly of a pragmatic nature. Just as in the pre-Christian communities, it is above all a question of political prestige and socio-economic security. Whereas the Papuans, however, ask directly for schools, hospitals and shops, the Melanesians are initially more concerned with the Christian ritual, through which they hope to achieve their socio-economic aims.

The influence of Christianity can be gathered from the image of the missionaries and catechists in particular, as well as from the enthusiastic almost unbounded conversion of the inhabitants (especially the Melanesians) to the Churches.

The first missionaries (and the colonial civil servants and traders too) were often regarded as ghostly bringers of culture or as returning forefathers. Even when the Melanesians and Papuans recognize that they are dealing with mortal men and not with spirits, they usually meet the missionaries with great awe (honour and fear), since they are convinced by their ritual knowledge and swayed by their material power. The native catechists and teachers, who share in the prestige of the overseas missionaries, take over to a certain extent the position of the traditional group elders. They understand too how to make their power effective in the pastoral and in the political sphere.

In this connection it should also be noted that in some areas rivalries arise between missionaries and colonial civil servants (especially on questions of marriage and schools) and leads to the development of a Church–State dualism.

Although it appears that a splendid success in conversions and promising advances towards civilization are being made and although the enthusiasm of the first Christians leads in many areas to the abandonment of social and religious customs, none the less we must make a few critical observations, at least from the ethnological point of view. Traditional culture has certainly changed in important aspects, but none the less the basic social and political structures and in particular the ritual pragmatism remain almost totally unaffected. Christian missionary work results simply in the exchange of traditional social and religious rites for Christian rites and elements of Western civilization. In other words: the Christian religion takes over the function of the old ideology based on goods and in this respect the community remains pagan.

III. Syncretistic Communities

After a few years of missionary work, mostly in the second generation of baptized, a certain disillusion becomes apparent. The communities think they have not reached, or have not reached quickly enough, what they hoped for from Christianity. These disillusioned new Christians suspect the missionaries and Europeans of concealing the real Christian or Western ritual.

This disillusion was expressed in the following way by a Christian catechist in pidgin, the language of communication: "We have become Christians, what's happened to the rice? Our children have gone to school, what's happened to the fish? You whites aren't hiding anything, are you?" In many districts the native population is withdrawing disillusioned from the missionaries; in isolated cases it even comes to the use of force. "Cargo talk" (talk about goods) and "cargo cult" (the cult of goods) sprout up everywhere, that is, the traditional goods ideology is activated in many palavers and the Christian communities try to overcome the dilemma by using syncretistic cult ceremonies.

The syncretism of the cargo cult, which is still prevalent over wide areas of Papua, can be seen in the religious as well as in the secular sphere. Here it is a case of ethnocentric and ritualistic interpretations of Christian doctrines and rites as well as of the educational, technical and political institutions.

In the religious sphere a blending of Christianity with the traditional religious ideas and rites takes place. The people and places in Old Testament events, as well as the birth and death of Christ, are transposed to Papua. In one case a Melanesian was even killed, as a black Christ, before the eyes of a bishop. The prophets of the goods cult receive instructions in visions from God or Christ about prayers, hymns and rites. They proclaim the new "road bilong cargo" (road to goods), social equality with Europeans and the return of the dead.

In the educational system it can be shown that at least in the initial stages the schools are regarded as agencies for the true occult knowledge ("save true"). The English language and mathematic formulae play a considerable role. Banks, cheques, big stores and the co-operative trading system are frequently imitated, as well as ships, aeroplanes and radio equipment, since it is believed that through these things the way or key ("ki") to goods can be found. Some cult leaders try to buy the cargo "secret" from the whites, and often arrange extortionate collections of money in the communities for this purpose.

In the political field, it is reported that members of the local council or of the national House of Assembly are elected in order to find out the occult law ("lo"). Technical parliamentary terms, such as "agenda", "poll", "law" and "independence", are pronounced reverently by adherents of the goods cult. Western ways of behaviour, military drill or national symbols, especially the flag, are new rites in the syncretistic cargo cult of the communities.

There is a great mass of excellent source material and literature on the subject of the cargo cult. It would range too widely here to go into further details or to document the reaction of the missionaries and government officials. It must suffice to reiterate that although a traumatic change has certainly taken place in many aspects of local culture, the cargo cult is by no means finished, but has found a new ritual, i.e. syncretistic, expression.

IV. LOCAL COMMUNITIES

In some districts, for instance on Manus Island and in Bougainville, cargo cult adherents have formed isolated communities, reminiscent of the "independent churches" in Africa. But in the other cargo cult movements, too, indeed even in areas where there are no active cults, ethnocentric and national ambitions, especially in the political field, are becoming obvious.

One of the cargo cult leaders, who is also a member of the House of Assembly, characterizes this development as follows: "There are two mountains in our country. First of all we have to climb these mountains, so that we know everything, then we shall remove the mountains." It is clear that the two mountains in question are the Australian Government and the Christian missions. The removal of the mountains means the preliminaries to independence and autonomy.

The pressure for independence and nationalism can be seen in the House of Assembly and even more clearly in the free independence movements, at the university in Port Moresby and also at the conference for native clergy. These movements, although certainly not free from emotionalism, have as their aim the establishment of the rights of self-determination, of independent initiative, of social equality and cultural self-sufficiency in State and Church.

It is interesting to note how in the legitimate nationalism of Papua the dualism of Church and State, as well as the secularization of the economy, politics and society makes itself felt more and more strongly. The Church is thus in danger of becoming a private parallel organization, concerned only with heaven and the saving of souls. At any rate there are already complementary movements, which demand that the Church should take on a political commitment too.

For a long time the institutional Church responded with "hands off politics". One step which contributed towards overcoming this attitude was the election of a European priest to the House of Assembly. In the meantime many secular and regular priests have made known their readiness to take part in the local councils.

The political commitment of the native clergy and native members of monastic orders is exceptionally strong and emotional. At any rate the danger of clericalism is recognized and was indeed expressed in discussions about the candidature of a native priest. Now the responsibility of the laity in Church and State is being emphasized more and more. The pastoral letter of the bishops of all Christian Churches in Papua, shortly to be published, may be regarded as an indication of this move. This pastoral letter deals with the imminent political independence, with questions of land reform, economic development and Christian eschatology. The preparation of this letter does not rest simply in the hands of the bishops' conference. Rather the bishops entrusted the working out of the document to several experts and consulted native as well as European priests and laymen.

Although it is still too early to evaluate developments, since the effects of the declaration of independence would have to be taken into account, it can none the less be seen already that a real cultural change and a change in the Christian community's political commitment is in process of taking place. The interplay of socio-political and religious forces develops for the present into a Church–State dualism, in which religion becomes a private matter and the economy as well as politics are secularized. In this way ritual pragmatism is certainly surmounted in principle, but it also means that any political commitment by the Christian communities is neutralized. The clericalism already evident in earlier community models rises to a peak in the local communities with the active political and parliamentary commitment of both overseas and native clergy. But other forces, which should be taken seriously, are now coming into play and these emphasize the political function of the layman in the Church. There is therefore good reason to hope for a legitimate localization, laicization, democratization and secularization of the Christian communities.

V. Critical Summary and Evaluation

1. It must be stressed that the four community models in Papua sketched above co-exist side by side and it is not simply a case of an historical development from ritualism and tribalism to secularization and nationalization throughout the whole country. The different times of contact with Europeans and a defective communications network have resulted in traditional, early Christian, syncretistic and local communities existing at the same time.

2. The vast majority of the communities in the highlands of Papua must be classified as early Christian. Most of the coastal and island communities are syncretistic, and in the towns, particularly in the Gazelle peninsula of New Britain, the development towards local communities has set in.

3. In those communities where a longer evolution of cultural contact can be historically documented, three historical phases are clearly recognizable—enthusiasm, disillusion and nationalism.

(a) In the phase of enthusiasm, the communities accept Western domination in politics, economics and Church, but interpret these according to their traditional materialistic ideology.

(b) Disillusion with the colonial government, economic dependence and ecclesiastical paternalism characterizes the second phase. The communities try to surmount this dilemma through syncretistic ritualism.

(c) With nationalism comes a very strong emotional rejection of colonial and ecclesiastical influence and simultaneously a dualistic and secular domination of communal life.

4. Any attempt at evaluating the political commitment of the communities ought not to be satisfied with representing phenomena such as ritualistic-pragmatic conversion in the early Christian community or the syncretism and dualism of subsequent community models as entirely negative and attributing them to the false aims, methods and expectations of the overseas missionaries. Rather the development must be seen from a cultural and historical point of view, that is, as the spiritual process of assimilating cultural contact and cultural change. In this spiritual and emotional conflict the community models and behaviour patterns described above are revealed as inherent.

5. That should not mean that the institutionalized missionary Church can be absolved from any guilt. For long enough the Church in Papua did not know how to recognize the role of ideology in the conversion and development process nor the danger of itself becoming an ideology. Critical and empirical assessments and corrections worked out in dialogue were introduced not long ago on a national basis with the project "Self-study of the Church in Papua, New Guinea".

6. Finally another problem, one easily overlooked by Western observers of missionary communities, should be pointed out. Models of pastoral care, liturgy and development politics are not immediately valid and applicable in Papua, since the cultural background and in particular the models and phases of the spiritual and emotional conflict are different in different places: the French and Marxist revolutions, although not without their effect on Papua, New Guinea, did not take place here.

Translated by Rosaleen Ockenden

Lukas Gämperle

Examples of Christian Political Commitment in Tanzania

IT WOULD be an understandable reaction to ask why Tanzania has been selected as an example of political commitment in Christian communities. Its inadequate state of development at the time of achieving independence in December 1961 and its natural disadvantages in mineral resources hardly predestined this particular country to come to the front of the international stage. Yet its orientation towards humanity and racial understanding subsequently highlighted Tanzania as an exemplary case of peaceful development. After a few years, however, many sympathizers became disillusioned with the country. They could not understand why Tanzania was also open to the East and even enjoyed very friendly relations with the People's Republic of China. But nowadays interest in Tanzania is very great in all those circles concerned for the well-being of the developing nations, since with its policy of solidarity and self-maintenance (*ujamaa na kujitegemea*), the country would seem to be pointing out a new way ahead for the developing nations.[1]

The Church in Tanzania is still young. The first missionaries reached the country little more than a century ago. Among the thirteen million inhabitants, there are now some two-and-a-half to three million Catholics, whereas the other Churches (prin-

[1] J. K. Nyerere, *Freedom and Unity: A Selection from Writings and Speeches, 1952–65* (Dar es Salaam, 1965); J. K. Nyerere, *Freedom and Socialism: A Selection from Writings and Speeches, 1965–67* (Dar es Salaam, 1968); K. E. Svendsen and M. Teisen, *Self-reliant Tanzania* (Dar es Salaam, 1969).

146

cipally Lutherans and Anglicans) account for one-and-a-half to two million. President Julius K. Nyerere, a believing Catholic, has for years been concerned that Christianity should not only be practised but lived. For a long time the official Church has not been able to understand his indirect and occasionally direct criticism in this regard.[2] It was not clear to the Church in what direction the Nyerere way would lead. Even today a considerable section of the almost entirely African hierarchy seems only faintly inclined to go along with him. Yet a few bishops, mainly young ones, are fully committed. They have recognized that Nyerere's development policy and the selfless devotion of individuals and of communities required in that policy are virtually patterned upon man as inspired by the Gospel. The primary concern of these bishops is therefore no longer so much the provision of funds from overseas for the extension of church structures, but the stimulation of the people of God entrusted to their care, to translate the message and commission of Christ into action in everyday life.

From the viewpoint of history, there are favourable bases for a socio-politically committed Church. From the very start the missions took up the struggle against sickness (hospitals), and ignorance (schools), and for the improvement of the legal status of women. The fight against poverty was also waged by the Church, although this battle proved much more difficult. In this respect it became clear that in many instances an unfortunate mistake was made in doing too much *for* people, and not enough *with* them.

It is quite obvious that there is no desire today for a Church of individual piety, but that what is wanted is a socially committed Church; not so much autonomous social institutions as the co-operative effort of church personnel in state institutions. President Nyerere has even expressly declared his wish that the social dimension of the Gospel should be revealed and impressed upon the faithful. This, it is hoped, would lead the individual Christian to a committed effort on behalf of his fellow men. For a country like Tanzania, that includes the very important task of awakening in people—and most especially in all those

[2] J. K. Nyerere, *Speech to the Maryknoll Congress in New York* (October 1970; Dar es Salaam, 1970).

who are directly engaged in public service (civil service, associations, the Party, and so on)—a sense of responsibility, of integrity and working discipline. It is obvious that the Christian community too must be prepared for commitment above all on this basis.

At the present moment, the influence in Tanzania of the average Christian parish on its environment is still far too ineffective. In many places in the past Christian initiation and education gave far too little evidence of this duty. Christianity was far too often acquired as a system, and not so much as good news and a spur to a new life.

Nevertheless there are many examples of how Christian communities tried—with varying persistence and not always successfully—to work for the improvement of the living conditions of their fellow men. The examples given here are by no means exhaustive. It is also quite possible that—unknown to the author—there are more impressive examples among the Christian parishes of Tanzania. For it is precisely in very recent years that numerous Christians have been touched by this concern.

In many parishes in the country, above all in the diocese of Bukoba, even before Independence, moves for political commitment in Christian communities emanated from groups of the Franciscan lay movement. The driving force here was a Bukoba teacher—Stanislaus Mutayabarwa. At the beginning of the sixties, with the help of the movement, he founded an action group to raise the living standard of the population. Centres were built in several villages where African retailers could obtain their goods at reasonable prices and where travellers could be sure of finding accommodation. The concern was unable to develop in accordance with the initiator's and his associates' hopes, above all because of the lack of trained and reliable personnel. Nevertheless, it did offer the people valuable help, especially in the influence it had on the pricing of major consumer goods.

In 1966 some Christians in the town parish of Msimbazi in Dar es Salaam took the initiative in setting up a loan-society. Closely connected with the parish and even called after it (the Msimbazi Parish Credit Union), the society was from the start quite open to non-Catholics in the parish area. Hence Christians and non-Christians alike are able to profit from this social in-

stitution. They have somewhere, where, without any great for-
malities, they are able to lodge their savings, and where they can
get loans on good terms to pay school fees or a bride-price, to
build a house, to improve their professional know-how, or for
some economic undertaking. There are quite a number of such
loan-societies in Tanzania. Originally they were the brain-child
of Joseph Mutayoba, a layman in the secretariat of the Bishops'
Conference. Then the Government also began to take an interest
in them and to promote them.

In Kilolero (diocese of Mahenge), far out in the bush, the local
Christian parish conducts a basically co-operative store. The purpose of this undertaking is to ensure that throughout the year,
and above all during the long rainy season, the people of the area
are supplied at appropriate prices with their most important
staples (sugar, salt, soap, paraffin, and so on). These co-operators
still rely very much on the parish priest's help. But the work
itself, that they carry out with him, is the best form of education
in social thought, collective work and the assumption of responsibility.

The same bush parish in Kilolero has undertaken other measures in the interests of the people and their basic daily existential
concerns. A co-operatively run maize mill not only makes their
work easier but guarantees them better nutrition, and hence
makes them better able to withstand sickness and to do their
work. In 1971 the parish decided to dig a village well, and made
initial provision for it in their annual budget. The plan was presented to the local government development committee with a
request for a contribution. Arrangements and measurements
were made without the people actually getting to use the desired
water supply. In the following year the well once again appeared
on the parish budget even though the goal was not reached.
Nevertheless the will is there to pursue the project until it is
realized, just as it has been in some other places. What water can
mean is known only to someone who has found himself in the
bush with his throat parched, longing for the stuff.

Even the care of the poor was undertaken by the Christians of
Kilolero. The church council examines requests for assistance
and, according to need, approves the granting of contributions
from parish funds. The initiative for road-building and a suspen-

sion bridge and this for a connection with the nearest market-town came largely from the parish priest, but his parishioners willingly co-operated and thus enabled a project to go forward that again serves the entire population of the area. In Ngoher-anga, a parish near to Kilolero, several years ago a training course for women was organized. The topics were pregnancy, birth and child-care. Since they came to see that much of what they had until then ascribed to spirits and sorcery had natural causes, these women decided to send two of their number for a course lasting some months in the nearest hospital, so that they could take over midwifery services for the entire neighbourhood.

In Ngoheranga, too, as in various other parishes in the diocese of Mahenge (Biro, Merera, Mpanga, Ruaha), for some time a tractor has been available for field preparation. The tractor be-longs to the parish, its use is controlled by a committee, and it is of course available for use by the whole population. Clearly this has meant a significant increase in cultivation and that better harvests can be scheduled. But, here again, it is also evident that people are being led to think and to bear responsibility socially.

In many places, hunger, which repeatedly afflicts whole neigh-bourhoods, is a major problem. Yet Merera is a good example of how this problem can be solved by an appropriate common effort. The Wandamba tribe are said to suffer famine every third year. But when, a short while ago, a group of European medical students visited the area, they found that the children of Merera were strikingly well-fed. That is certainly attributable to the im-proved and more regular harvests of the last few years. How were these achieved? The parish priest and his helpers persuaded the villagers to join a co-operative group. Together they prepared their fields near the village. With ditches and barbed wire they protected the fields against wild beasts and finally dug a channel so that during the rainy seasons the floods of the nearby river would be kept away from the rice fields. The successful battle against beasts and water, and the labour in common, together with cultivation at the right time, have visibly improved the economic status and health of the population.

In the Ruaha area, it has been as long as anyone can remember a fatalistic expectation that the rainy season would transform the plains of the valley into a quagmire, and that the road leading over the plain should be made impassable from time to time. This situation was brought to an end by the efforts of the local Christian community. In the dry season they set themselves to erect a sufficiently high and solid dam over which the valley road could pass. In this way the entire population were liberated from the annual recurrence of extreme distress.

Maua in the diocese of Moshi is one of the very many examples of the Christians of a locality opening the way to increased educational possibilities for the whole population. Although school attendance is unusually high in the thickly populated Wachagga territory, in Maua for instance a hundred children reaching school age each year find there is no place for them. The parish contribution is to have taken the first steps to ensure that the four existing primary schools were extended, and that a further educational establishment was opened for girls leaving school.

The Christian parishes of the dioceses of Kigoma and Rulenge, and their forward-looking Bishops Nsabi and Mwoleka, deserve collective mention. The political commitment of the Christians, understood as devotion to their fellow men and concern for their improved ability to master their life situations, seems to be especially strong there. Parishes act on the government-launched idea of communal villages (*ujamaa* villages); prominent parishioners, for example even catechists, undertake leading tasks in such villages. Here one has the impression that the Christian communities are wholly concerned to devote themselves to the national development policy. The faithful are concerned to co-operate on development projects, but to offer constructive criticism, and to influence the associated decisions in accordance with their best knowledge and in the interest of the case.

As a whole, the Christians of Tanzania are becoming increasingly aware that faith in Christ is not simply a matter of pious devotion. It is a question of devoting oneself in accordance with Christ's words to one's fellow man: to one's fellow man who hungers, thirsts and does not know how to protect himself from sicknesses, and whose intellectual and physical abilities are lying fallow. But for the road from knowledge to action, someone is still needed to stimulate and lead: whether a priest, the church council, a sister, or individual committed laymen.

Translated by John Griffiths

Biographical Notes

HUGO ASSMANN was born in 1933. Doctor of theology (Gregorian University), he has studied sociology and is a former co-ordinator of the Institute of Theology of São Paulo and a visiting professor at the University of Münster. He is now secretary of studies of "Church and Society in Latin America", Santiago de Chile. Among his published works are three small books of the pastoral type (Brazil); *El sacramento de la penitencia en la Teología actual*; *Diskussion zur Theologie der Revolution*, in collaboration (Munich, 1969); *Opresión-Liberación. Desafió a los cristianos* (Montevideo, 1971); and *Teoponta: Una experiencia guerrillera* (Oruro, 1971; Caracas, 1972). He is also co-author of *América Latina: Movilización popular y fe cristiana* (Bogotá, 1971) and of *Pueblo oprimido, señor de la historia* (Montevideo, 1972).

BERTRAND DE CLERCQ was born in 1932 and ordained in the Dominican Order in 1958. Doctor of philosophy (Louvain) and licentiate in political and social sciences, he has taught philosophy and social ethics at the University of Louvain since 1963, principally to the Faculty of Social Sciences. He is also editor of *Tijdschrift voor Filosofie* and of *Kultuurleven*. Among his published works is *Godsdienst en ideologie in de politiek*, which has been translated into French, German, Spanish, Italian and Czech. He has also contributed articles, mainly on political problems and social ethics, to many reviews.

YVAN DANIEL was born in 1909 in Nîmes and ordained in 1935. He studied at the Sorbonne, Saint-Sulpice and at the Institut Catholique, Paris. Licentiate in canon law, he has been parish priest of Saint Pierre-Saint Paul and dean of Ivry and is now parish priest of Saint Germain de Charonne and dean of the 20th district of Paris. Among his published works are: *La France, pays de mission?* in collaboration with Henri Godin (Paris, 1943); *L'équipement paroissial d'un diocèse urbain: Paris* (Paris, 1957); *Vivre en chrétien dans mon quartier* (Paris, 1943–1967); and one of the adaptations of the "Catéchisme national français", *Chrétiens partout* (Paris, 1968).

ROBERT DELANEY was born in 1930 in Los Angeles. He was a volunteer for pastoral work and the development of the community in Mexico from 1965 to 1968. In 1969 he commenced his doctoral studies in theology at Tübingen and completed them in Münster. He has contributed to *Neue*

Gemeindemodelle (1971) and will shortly publish his doctoral dissertation on San Miguelito, Panama.

LUKAS GÄMPERLE, O.F.M.cap., was born in 1928 in Bütschwil (Switzerland) and ordained in 1953. He studied at Innsbruck, Solothurn (Studium of his Order), Fribourg and Oxford. He is working on the missions and for more than ten years has been director of the Social Centre of Msimbazi in Dar es Salaam. Since 1970 he has been Vicar General of the Archdiocese of Dar es Salaam.

JOSÉ-MARIA GONZÁLEZ-RUIZ was born in 1916 in Seville and ordained in 1939. He is *Canónigo Lectoral* of Málaga Cathedral and professor of the New Testament at the Higher Institute of Pastoral Studies in Madrid. Among his principal published works are: *San Pablo, Cartas de la Cautividad* (Madrid, 1956); *Epístola de San Pablo a los Gálatas* (Madrid, 1971²); *El cristianismo no es un humanismo* (1970³); *Pobreza evangélica y promoción umana* (Barcelona, 1970³); *Marxismo y cristianismo frente al hombre nuevo* (Madrid, 1972⁴); *Dios es gratuito, pero no superflue* (Madrid, 1971); *Dios está en la base* (Barcelona, 1971); *Ay de mí si no evangelizare* (Bilbao, 1972²). Most of these have been translated into French and Italian.

NORBERT GREINACHER was born in 1931 in Freiburg im Breisgau and ordained in 1956. He studied in Freiburg, Paris and Vienna. Doctor of theology (1955), he is professor of pastoral theology at the University of Tübingen. Among his published works are: *Die Kirche in der städtischen Gesellschaft* (Mainz, 1966); *Bilanz des deutschen Katholizismus* (Mainz, 1966), in collaboration with H. Th. Risse; *Soziologie der Pfarrei* (Freiburg, 1955); *Die deutsche Priesterfrage* (Mainz, 1961), with J. Dellepoort and W. Menges; *Regionalplanung in der Kirche* (Mainz, 1965), with E. Bodzenta and L. Grond; *Zugehörigkeit zur Kirche* (Mainz, 1964), with W. Menges; *Priestergemeinschaften* (Mainz, 1960); *Die Funktion der Theologie in Kirche und Gesellschaft* (Munich, 1969), with P. Lengsfeld; and *In Sache Synode* (Düsseldorf, 1970), with K. Lang.

NORMANN HEPP, who is 34 years old, studied philosophy and theology at Munich and Freising. Since 1967 he has been working as a priest in Munich and district. He is a member of a group with the task of organizing an ecclesial communitarian, social and formation centre in a subsidiary town of Munich of 80,000 people. He is co-author of *Denkschrift zur Gemeindearbeit* (Munich, 1969), editor of *Neue Gemeindemodelle* (Vienna, 1971) and author of a notable article "Kirchliche Sozial- und Bildungsarbeit in einer Trabantenstadt", in *Diakonia*, 3 (1972).

HERMANN JANSSEN, M.S.C., was born in 1933 in Ostfriesland (Germany) and was ordained in 1960. He studied philosophy and theology at the major schools of his Order, ethnology, sociology and philosophy at the Universities of Cologne and Vienna (Ph.D. 1966). In 1963–64 he was engaged in research in Central India; in 1967 he made study trips to the Indies, the Philippines and New Guinea. From 1967 to 1969 he did pastoral and ethnological work in Melanesia and since 1969 he has been director of the Melanesian Institute for Pastoral and Socio-Economic Service. He is also founder of and contributor to *Catalyst*, a social and pastoral review for Melanesia in which articles by him on the Church in Melanesia have appeared in 1971 and 1972. In 1971 he made further study trips to East and West Africa.

KLEMENS RICHTER was born in 1940 in Leipzig. Licentiate in theology, doctor of theology (1972) in the domain of Catholic theology in Münster, he is also a scientific assistant for the science of liturgy and an academic counsellor. His work is mainly concerned with pastoral aspects of liturgy, formation of adults and questions of the Church in a socialist society. Among his published works are articles in *Bibel und Liturgie, Diakonia, Stimmen der Zeit, Orientierung, Publik* and *Jahrb. für christl. Socialwiss*; radiophonic contributions on the situation of the Church in the German Democratic Republic; *Neue Totenliturgie* (Essen, 1971[3]); *Die Feier der Trauung* (Essen, 1971[3]); *Die Trauung in der Gemeinde* (Essen, 1972) and *Die Feier der Krankenkommunion* (Essen, 1972).

LUDWIG RÜTTI was born in 1936 in Emmenbrücke (Switzerland) and ordained in 1962. He studied at the Seminary of the Missions, Schöneck (Switzerland) and at the University of Münster, where he gained his doctorate in theology in 1971. He has been scientific collaborator at the Missionswissenschaftlich Institut of the University of Münster and is now bursar of the Deutsche Forschungsgemeinschaft. Among his published works is *Zur Theologie der Mission—Kritische Analysen und neue Orientierungen* (1972).

EDWARD SCHILLEBEECKX, O.P., was born in 1914 in Antwerp and ordained in 1941. He studied at the Dominican Faculty of Theology of the Saulchoir, and at the Ecole des Hautes Etudes at the Sorbonne. Doctor of theology (1951) and master of theology (1959), he has been professor of dogmatic theology at the University of Nijmegen since 1958 and a visiting professor at Harvard University; he is also editor-in-chief of *Tijdschrift voor Theologie*. Among his published works are: *Openbaring en theologie; God en mens; Wereld en Kerk; De zending van der Kerk; Geloofsverstaan: Interpretatie en kritiek*; and *God, the Future of Man*.

THEODORE M. STEEMAN, O.F.M., was born in Rotterdam in 1928 and ordained in 1953. He studied sociology at the University of Leyden and religion and society at Harvard University, and now teaches sociology of religion and Christian social ethics at Boston College, U.S.A. Among his published works are: *The Sociology of Atheism* (Rome, 1967) and "The Underground Church: Forms and Dynamics of Change in Contemporary Catholicism" in *Religious Situation 1969* (Boston, 1969), which has been translated into French and Italian.

MICHAEL TRABER was born in 1929 in Zürich and was ordained in 1956 as a member of the Society of Swiss Missions of Bethlehem. He studied theology at the Seminary of the Missions, Schöneck-Beckenried, and sociology and the science of communications at Fordham University and the University of New York (Ph.D., 1960). He was director of the Communication Centre "Mambo Press" at Gwelo, Rhodesia, from 1961 to 1970. He is now *docent* at the Confederate Higher Technical School at Zürich and president of the National Swiss Commission Iustitia et Pax. Among his published works are: *Schweiz—Dritte Welt* (Zürich/Fribourg, 1971); *Rassismus und weisse Vorherrschaft* (Nuremberg/Fribourg, 1971); and *Das revolutionäre Afrika* (Nuremberg/Fribourg, 1972).